What Online Marketing Executives Are Saying About *Manager's Guide to Online Marketing*

Finally, a handbook for managers in this new era of online marketing—including social and mobile. This has been a long time coming and is an essential guide to the many high-leverage opportunities available to managers. Andy Grove always wrote about management leverage, and in this age you can be more efficient and effective than ever if you know how to use the tools.

—**Brett Hurt**, Founder
President and CEO, Bazaarvoice, Inc.

In an era where online social relationships influence purchase decisions, this book serves as a critical reference tool to help online marketers navigate across social media channels and in a manner that drives measurable results. A must-read for anyone wanting to better optimize his marketing investments.

—**Lisa Bacus**
Executive VP & CMO
American Family Insurance

Millions of people every day use Foursquare on their phones to connect with friends, businesses, and brands around the world. This book provides specific strategies on how to leverage location-based technologies for your company. I highly recommend *Manager's Guide to Online Marketing.*

—**Steven Rosenblatt**
Chief Revenue Officer, Foursquare

Just when marketers thought they had "digital" figured out, the web changed and has become social, mobile, and more pervasive than ever. Jason's work on *Manager's Guide to Online Marketing* clearly lays out what's different this time around and how marketing managers need to rethink their digital strategies and tactics. This is one book custom tailored for marketing professionals looking to move the needle in a digital world.

—**David Armano**
Managing Director
Edelman Digital Central Region

As companies look to build their online and social media marketing initiatives, Jason Weaver carefully outlines each step to achieving success in *Manager's Guide to Online Marketing*. Important topics around developing a web communication policy, regulating and controlling social media within a large organization, and identifying and understanding how to deal with online legal issues are all covered in this book. It's a must-read for every manager involved in this area.

—**Sandy Carter**
IBM Vice President
Social Business Evangelism
and Sales

Manager's Guide to Online Marketing

Manager's Guide to Online Marketing

Jason D. Weaver
Founder and CEO, Shoutlet, Inc.

McGraw-Hill
New York Chicago San Francisco Lisbon
London Madrid Mexico City Milan New Delhi
San Juan Seoul Singapore Sydney Toronto

The McGraw-Hill Companies

1 2 3 4 5 6 7 8 9 0 QFR/QFR 1 8 7 6 5 4 3

ISBN 978-0-07-180187-4
MHID 0-07-180187-1

e-ISBN 978-0-07-180188-1
e-MHID 0-07-180188-X

This is a CWL Publishing Enterprises book developed for McGraw-Hill by CWL Publishing Enterprises, Inc., Madison, Wisconsin, www.cwlpub.com.

This book is printed on acid-free paper.

Contents

Acknowledgments

Being surrounded by great people brought me several amazing opportunities in my life. This book is one of those opportunities. There are countless people to thank for helping me complete this book, first and foremost, Barry Callen, author of *Manager's Guide to Marketing, Advertising, and Publicity*. Without Barry, there would be no book. Thank you for recommending me for the assignment. John Woods (CWL Publishing Enterprises, the packager of this book). I appreciate your patience and valuable insights throughout this endeavor. Lili Beck and Jocelyn Godfrey kept this book moving for me every single day—both spending countless hours editing my chapters.

There are many people I need to thank at Shoutlet: David Prohaska, without whom I might not have written this book. You knew how badly I wanted to do this project, and you gave me the opportunity. To the entire executive management team: Aaron Everson, Tarik Hart, Eric Christopher, and David Prohaska, thanks once again for allowing me to write most of this book while continuing my "day job." To my team at Shoutlet: Kara Martens, Rachel Madden, Carly Rudeen, Jason Konen, Blake Samic, and David McKnight: for keeping me on my toes and up to date with the ever-changing social media landscape. A huge thank-you to each and every one of Shoutlet's customers for believing in my dream and always letting me try new ideas. Much of this book is based on what I learned and experienced from working on your campaigns.

I could not do any of this without the support of my family. Thanks to my parents, Linda and Bob Luther and Dale and Mary Weaver, for always encouraging me to go where others wouldn't dare. My three beautiful children, Oliver, Stellina, and Sullivan, thank you for letting your dad work on this book when I could have been playing with you.

Finally, I'd like to especially thank my wife, Alexias Weaver, who is my angel—a gift from heaven. It's only with your continued encouragement and support that I'm able to follow my dreams. I love you.

This book is dedicated to my late grandfather, Walter Robinson. I wish you could see how the days you let me play on your computers while you were at IBM for 35 years have inspired me to go into the world of technology and do what I love. I miss you.

Introduction

Online marketing has changed significantly since my first job managing websites for JBL in 1997. About half of the companies that you come in contact with today didn't have websites back then, let alone a blog or social media presence. Over the next few years Google would come onto the scene and change search forever. Marketing on the web soon became a complex mixture of mathematical search formulas.

Fast forward to today. Now we have more options than ever to get our message in front of people. Platforms like Facebook, YouTube, and Twitter help brands stay connected to fans and followers. Google still leads search and is trying to master social media, too. Mobile options are too numerous to mention, and services like Foursquare, Pinterest, and Voxer are fighting to be your platform of choice. Online marketing can seem like an overwhelming task.

Since keeping up with the pace of social networks, web-based marketing tools, and the newest strategies can be difficult, I wrote this book to provide you with the building blocks to master this medium and help you to hone your skills as the online world moves ahead. This book provides everything, from the fundamentals of online marketing to advanced tactics for the seasoned online marketing veteran. It is written to be a resource that you can turn to each time you plan an online strategy.

Whenever I train new employees or clients in social media, I tell them that they first must understand the basics. I feel it's important to know the history of online marketing before you can begin to understand its future. Therefore, Chapters 1, 2, and 3 take you through the basics. You'll learn about both Web 1.0 and now Web 2.0 and social media. These chapters give you in-depth information about companies that have forever changed the way we transmit information and ideas among one another. I recommend reading these chapters even if you think you already know this stuff, for there is real value in going back to study the beginning.

Most mistakes I've seen made in online marketing are the result of companies diving in without doing the necessary research. So if you are looking for strategies and tactics that you can begin using today, I recommend skipping ahead to Chapters 5, 6, and 9. These chapters will save you both time and money by helping you pinpoint your target audience and by developing a measurable campaign. Chapter 5 takes you through the planning process. Chapter 6 evaluates marketing tools that will make your job easier, while Chapter 9 provides specific strategies based on your business type.

If you want to become a social media guru or you are trying to gain enough attention to land your dream job in online marketing, I recommend reading Chapter 4 on personal branding. This chapter provides information on social networks, online communities, and influencer rating tools that must be included as a part of your online marketing arsenal.

If you're working for a large company and need to find a starting point, Chapter 10 provides detailed plans for building an online team, regulating and controlling your brand, and establishing a web communication policy. Chapter 7 gives you the tools you'll need to execute your company's internal communication strategies. Chapter 8 explains how to make sales using social media. Finally, Chapters 11 and 12 provide some ideas about the future of online marketing and how to stay ahead of the curve.

There is no silver bullet in online marketing. Successful online campaigns are a careful balance of messaging, technology, and research. You have to be willing to "build the airplane as you're flying it" by refining your strategy as you go. You have to be maneuverable and willing to take calculated risks to master online marketing. When done correctly there are millions to be made online.

Special Features

Titles in the Briefcase Books series are designed to give you practical information written in a friendly, person-to-person style. The chapters deal with tactical issues and include lots of examples. They also feature numerous sidebars that give you different types of specific information. Here's a description of the sidebars you'll find in this book.

Every subject has some jargon, including this one, dealing with online marketing. These sidebars provide definitions of terms and concepts as they are introduced.

These sidebars do just what their name suggests: give you tips to intelligently apply the strategies and tactics described in this book to effectively implement your online marketing plan.

Tricks of the Trade sidebars give you insider how-to hints on techniques astute managers use to execute the tactics described in this book.

It's always useful to have examples that show how the principles in the book are applied. These sidebars provide those, along with case studies of the use and implementation of online marketing.

Caution sidebars provide warnings for where things could go wrong when undertaking your online marketing plans.

How can you make sure you won't make a mistake when you're trying to implement the techniques the book describes? You can't, but these sidebars give you practical advice on how to minimize the possibility of things going wrong.

This icon identifies sidebars where you'll find specific applications and websites that you can use to put your online marketing strategies to work and measure the success of your efforts.

Manager's Guide to Online Marketing

Benefits of Effective Online Marketing

Everyone wants their business to have an online presence. Whether you work in retail, run a company that sells to other businesses, or manage a nonprofit organization, we all want to be found online. Most companies continuously strive to achieve the highest placement they can on Google and other search engines. With the explosion of social media, many companies also want to increase the number of their Facebook fans, Twitter followers, and YouTube subscribers. Chances are, if you are running a company or a nonprofit organization, you want to make or raise money. Every company's leaders want to speed the rate at which they attract customers. This book aims to help you uncover ways to achieve your online business goals.

Before we go farther, it's important to note that every company has a different definition of success when it comes to online marketing. For retail companies that sell online, success is often defined by the number of transactions (direct sales) that take place on their e-commerce site. For an alcohol company, selling directly online in the United States is illegal, so its definition of success is increased brand recognition with the goal of increasing offline sales. For a nonprofit organization, success is defined by an increase in donations or new volunteers. Finally, for a company that sells professional services (banking, law, consulting), success is defined by the number of direct leads that translate into consultation sales offline.

GET THEM TALKING

Ideally, you want your customers to talk about you online in such a way that it improves your reputation while increasing your business.

BUILD IT AND THEY WILL COME ... OR WILL THEY?

Building a website is a crucial step in generating online business, but it isn't enough. You also need to take specific steps to ensure your website can be found by the people who would buy the products or services you offer.

Though each of these examples has a different objective, each can benefit from an increased online presence. Having a solid online marketing strategy can both increase awareness of your organization and make money for you.

Reduced Costs and Increased Efficiency

You've probably purchased this book for one of two reasons: either you are new to online marketing or you're uncertain about the value you're getting from your current online marketing efforts. The right online strategy can reduce costs from both advertising and operational standpoints. Companies like Procter & Gamble are shifting a large portion of their offline advertising and marketing budgets to online strategies. You can reduce your traditional marketing costs by examining some of your existing marketing tactics based on a few comparisons.

For example, I recently met with the marketing team of a health insurance company in my hometown. They were new to online marketing but interested in discovering how it could help them obtain more business (sell health insurance policies). Historically, their company had used the traditional means of radio, television, billboards, and print media.

I was curious to learn if they were effectively reaching their target audience with traditional advertising. Prior to our first meeting, I called the local television and radio stations and billboard companies to get a sense of cost per media impression. I was surprised to find out how expensive it was to reach the insurance company's target audience. I was even more surprised to discover that the company had no effective way to measure media impressions or their return on investment (ROI).

I began to build my case for online marketing to this company around the benefits of taking a large portion of the advertising budget and putting it online.

> **ROI (return on investment)** This is a factor frequently analyzed in marketing. Promotions that bring the highest response for the money spent are considered the most effective.
>
> **KEY TERMS**
>
> **Media impression** (in the context of online advertising) A measure of the number of times an ad is displayed. In online marketing, this refers to how many times the ad appears on a website, whether it is clicked on or not. Each time an ad displays, it counts as one impression.
>
> Counting impressions is the method by which most web advertising is accounted and paid for, and the cost is quoted in CPM (cost per thousand) impressions. Contrast CPM with CPC (cost-per-click), which is click-based, not impression-based.

This company's target audience for new insurance policies was a small business owner who had the authority to switch health insurance providers. I challenged the company with a simple set of questions that addressed the effectiveness of their conversion formula: How much was it costing them to reach their target audience today? The company was advertising on bill-boards in a city of only 300,000 people. They were paying $5,000 per month to advertise on the billboards. I asked, "Of the 300,000 people, do you know how many pass by the billboard each day?" Digging further, I asked, "How many are actually looking at the billboard?" But most important, "How many of those people who actually see the billboard are your target audience of small business owners who can decide to change health insurance providers?" The truth was out. They had no way to measure who was seeing their billboards or how effective those ads were in reaching small business owners. Nor did they have a concept of what kind of sales increase the promotion was giving them.

Over the next several meetings with the insurance company marketing team, I outlined a specific plan for an online strategy.

It was easy to illustrate the benefits of online marketing for the health insurance company by our second meeting. Their ROI with the billboards, television and radio commercials, and print ads did not yield the positive results they needed. I was able to design a specific plan for them

Why Billboards Aren't Always Better

With many traditional advertising channels—such as billboards—we have no way to track who sees or responds to a promotion. With online marketing, we can connect directly with our target audience while measuring results in real time. Whether you're trying to reach an international audience or simply a handful of people in your hometown, online marketing can be an effective approach to increasing sales and awareness. There are clear benefits to using online marketing to promote your products, services, business, or yourself.

that would target their potential customers more effectively and cost much less than traditional advertising methods.

Online advertising provides more maneuverability than traditional advertising. For example:

- You can "turn on a dime" with online marketing. You can update the sites you advertise on, change your message strategy, and cut or increase spending within minutes.

Calculating Your Marketing ROI

For marketing ROI, the tricky part is determining what constitutes your *return*, and what is your true investment. For example, different marketers might consider the following for the return:

- Total revenue generated by a campaign (or gross receipts or turnover, depending on your organization type and location, which is the top-line sales generated by the campaign).
- Gross profit, or a gross profit estimate, which is revenue minus the cost of goods (COG) to produce/deliver a product or service. Many marketers use the company's COG percentage—which is the average percentage for COG—(say 30 percent) and deduct it from the total revenue.
- Net profit, which is gross profit minus additional overhead expenses.

On the investment side, it's easy for marketers to input the media costs as the investment. But what other costs should you include? To execute your campaign, you might have:

- Creative costs
- Printing costs
- Technical costs (such as e-mail platforms, website coding, etc.)
- Management time
- Cost of sales

- Opposite of online marketing, once you place a print ad, run a television or radio commercial, or create a billboard, you are committed by contract to your message and the amount you spend, and you must wait through the publishing or broadcast dates before assessing results and readjusting strategy.

> **Top-line** Gross sales or revenues as opposed to bottom-line, which refers to the net income left after deducting expenses.
>
> 
>

When comparing traditional marketing with online marketing, it's easy to see the cost benefits and time savings. I also prefer online marketing because of the amount of targeting and measurement it provides. When I am able to track every movement of my marketing campaign, I don't just think—*I know*—how it's performing and whom it's reaching.

> SMART MANAGING
>
> **Test, Test, Test**
>
> Advertising and marketing managers are told to "test, test, test." They test modalities, markets, and methods—analyzing the ROI to determine where to reinvest. Online marketing holds an advantage over traditional marketing in that it provides in-depth and often instant measurement—making the "test, test, test" adage easier to achieve.

Increased Awareness

Almost all the companies I meet with want to get to "the sale" immediately with online marketing. Outside of the direct sale, there is a benefit of simply increasing your brand presence online for a sale that may occur later.

Truthfully, I had never had much interest in branding until I started my own company. I had always worked on the search engine optimization (SEO) and e-commerce aspects of marketing, so I wasn't involved in branding activities.

It wasn't until I started to experiment with social media that I began to understand the concepts of brand association and building relationships. Working with my clients, I experienced the result of first building a relationship with potential future customers via branding before moving to the transaction (sale) phase.

KEY TERMS

Brand Name, term, design, symbol, or any other feature that identifies one seller's good or service as distinct from those of other sellers. Branding also refers to the psychological aspects associated with a company or product—how it makes people think or feel.

The term "branding" originated with the hot iron markings used by ranchers to distinguish ownership of their cattle.

Search engine optimization (SEO) The process of optimizing your website to enhance its position through a natural (or organic) return from a popular search engine, such as Yahoo!, Google, or Bing. Companies continuously try to improve their search *ranking* (appearing higher on a search return page than other companies) to make themselves more visible.

We discuss search engine optimization, pay-per-click, social media, and content marketing in the next few chapters. You'll begin to understand how each tactic requires a different approach. Before you invest in online marketing, it is important to understand the rules of engagement for each online marketing strategy, as each is different in how it works tactically and technically.

For now, I'd like to share an example to illustrate how online marketing can work wonders. I like to talk about this next client when I'm giving marketing speeches, as people find it funny that a company would want to target irritable bowel syndrome (IBS) sufferers via online marketing. As I mentioned earlier, everyone is online. Visit lifeinabathroom.wordpress.com if you need proof.

FOR EXAMPLE

An Apple by Any Other Name

During the late 1980s and early 1990s, Apple experienced a huge boost when Pepsi marketing executive John Scully joined the company and increased the advertising budget from $15 million to $100 million—but more important, helped turn Apple into not just a product—but a brand. "People talk about technology, but Apple was a marketing company," Sculley told the *Guardian* newspaper in 1997. "It was the marketing company of the decade." The Apple brand enjoys tremendous loyalty among its customers—who consider Apple synonymous with innovation, creativity, and usability. Many consider Apple as the quintessential example of successful branding—in that the company has built a strong, positive brand association with its customers. (Source: Kahney, L., "Apple: It's All About the Brand," *Wired*, December 4, 2002.)

This particular client I worked with was indeed trying to reach people with IBS online to sell its medicinal product. Doing a "batch and blast" approach of distributing coupons wouldn't work with this audience. Many of these sufferers have tried several medications without success. The company knew that it had to build trust before a sale could occur. It wasn't until we researched the target audience that we found most IBS sufferers will do anything they can to avoid medication. So how does a company that sells IBS medication reach an audience that typically avoids it? The answer was that the company first needed to focus on building an online relationship with IBS sufferers before moving to the transaction phase.

A great deal of useful information came from the research. One finding we focused on was that people with IBS are typically instructed by their doctors to change their eating habits before taking medication. This was the obvious first step in interacting with IBS sufferers. With this finding, the company decided to provide healthy recipes and eating tips for people with IBS. Over the course of a few months, the company became a trusted source for IBS sufferers. It offered samples of its product, then coupons for purchases. It wasn't too long after it launched the initial branding campaign that people were "transacting," or buying, the product online.

The company only had to initiate the online relationship during a 90-

TRICKS OF THE TRADE

Think Relationship Before Sale

When building an online customer base, consider that customer loyalty will be stronger if you build a relationship before expecting sales. You wouldn't go to a new neighbor's house and ask to borrow a cup of flour the day he moves in from out of state. You'd build a relationship first through authentic dialogue and acts of neighborliness—such as bringing a batch of cookies, offering to watch his dog, telling him about the best home repair businesses in the area, or shooting the breeze over a glass of lemonade. Similarly in online marketing, your sales conversion rate will be higher if you first engage with customers through the content or service you provide. One way to foster engagement is through building a content base to help your customers. An advantage of using this approach is that it allows you to target your content to SEO—attracting the type of readers who are apt to convert to customers for your products or services.

day period to build online awareness and trust between the company and IBS sufferers. After the IBS sufferers felt a positive relationship had been established with the company, they began to share their recipes and stories with other IBS sufferers.

Figure 1-1 shows the phases of building a relationship before asking for a sale online.

- **Phase 1: Provide value.** Do this by giving useful information to the web visitor. In the case of IBS, the information was free recipes.
- **Phase 2: Interact and engage.** Ask your web visitors to engage with you through a contest, entry form, etc. With IBS, the company asked visitors to submit recipes of their own to share with other IBS sufferers.
- **Phase 3: Transact.** Now that you've built a relationship, it's appropriate to ask for the sale by offering a coupon or limited offer.

Once these phases are complete, you should see an audience of people with influence begin to share the offer with their friends.

Back when I published a magazine, we used the term *pass-along rate* (the number of times a magazine was shared with other readers). Publishers often bragged about how high their pass-along rates were when compar-

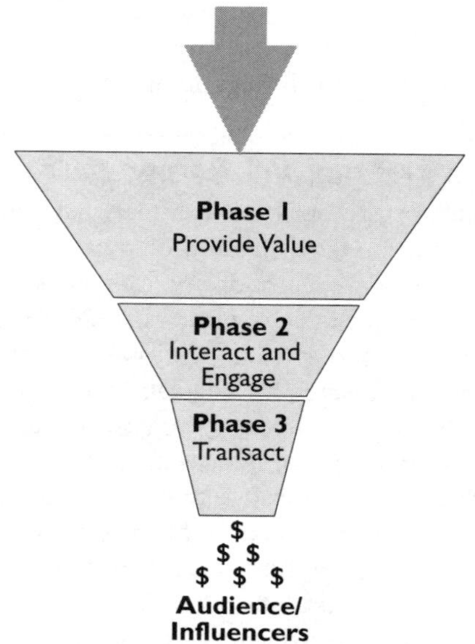

Figure 1-1. The phases of building an online relationship

ing themselves against their competitors. The web has a significantly higher pass-along rate than publications due to the ease with which information can be shared. The pass-along rate for web content can be tracked, so it's easy for you to know how many times your content is being shared as opposed to having a magazine publisher's representatives tell you how many times they think it is being shared.

The Shelf Life of a Web Campaign

There is a residual effect that happens once you've mastered online advertising and marketing that does not typically happen with traditional advertising. Today with the help of social networks, blogs, and e-mail, it's not uncommon for good web campaigns to get passed along well after your advertising spend has ended.

The lesson I learned early on when putting together an online marketing strategy is that research is the key to success. There is no better way to find out what your customers are doing online than to *ask them*. So many organizations I have worked with spend wasteful amounts of money figuring out their strategy as they go. In chapter 5, we go into how to plan, research, and align your online marketing expectations.

Pass-along rate How frequently a paid copy of a magazine (either by subscription or newsstand) is passed along to another person to read.

Improved Customer Service

For companies that sell online, customer service responsiveness is everything. Several companies have suffered public relations debacles by not responding quickly enough to a comment or complaint on Twitter, a blog, or a website, allowing the comment/com-

CAUTION

Social Media = Instant Unpaid Publicity

Today's smartphones allow customers to tweet instant updates about their experiences with your business. This provides a huge boon to you if their reports are positive—or potentially closes your doors if their reports are poor. Provide consistent and exemplary service so customers will only be tempted to brag about you online, rather than berate you.

plaint to become a real problem. Now more than ever, companies must prepare themselves to address customer service issues online and at lightning speed.

The lines connecting marketing, public relations, and customer service are becoming more blurred daily. Facebook, Twitter, and blogs have moved beyond simple social media sites to boast about your products and services into a complete online customer interaction with your brand. In today's high-tech world, you can search, buy, and complain about a product all during one interaction. Companies that embrace this change are quickly turning challenges into opportunities.

FOR EXAMPLE

CONTACTING COMCAST

Comcast Cable has historically been known for its poor customer service. Getting a customer support agent on the phone from Comcast was quite a task. That all changed when Frank Eliason of Comcast began the company's customer service response account on Twitter (www.businessweek.com/managing/content/jan2009/ca20090113_373506.htm). Eliason was able to turn a crisis into an opportunity in a way that Comcast had never seen before. He provided immediate responses to common cable support questions that were public for others to see, since customers often have similar support issues. Eliason recently published a book about his Comcast experience, *@ Your Service*, which can be purchased on Amazon.com (amzn.com/dp/1118217225).

Tips for Social Media Customer Service

Initiating social media customer service holds many advantages, as shown in the sidebar about Comcast. Social media customer service is instant, and it gives customers the chance to interact and spread messages virally.

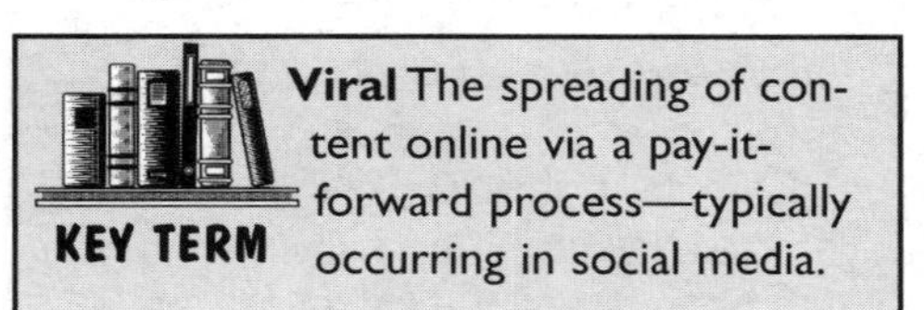

KEY TERM

Viral The spreading of content online via a pay-it-forward process—typically occurring in social media.

Social media customer service, however, comes with a unique set of opportunities—and challenges—in that once spread by users, it can stick around for years. Apply these three simple tips on a consistent basis to ensure that you are building positive rapport at all times in your social media efforts:

1. **Be authentic.** Make certain when you respond to customers on social media platforms that you are honest and factual. It only takes seconds for someone to find out what's actually behind the scenes in any organization.
2. **Be humble.** Remember, these are your customers and they want to know that you'll solve their issues. I have seen customer service representatives become confrontational when they get frustrated with a customer. Social media leaves quite a "paper trail," in that words written onto websites can stick around for years and get picked up by search engines—potentially hurting you with future customers who research your business. You should feel lucky to have these people as customers whether or not they are tough to deal with.
3. **Respond quickly.** I've found that social media users tend to be impatient. You'll need a full-time, dedicated customer service person if you are going to provide online support. Customers are quickly frustrated if they don't hear from you within about an hour.

Customer service based in social media shouldn't be customers' only option. Phone and e-mail support are also important options in case they don't see a social media response mechanism on a social site. However, social media can provide a rapid response system and often save companies money over a call center.

Be Careful with Social Media Support

CAUTION

It's imperative that you do not begin offering customer support through social media (Twitter, Facebook, YouTube) unless you can support it on an ongoing basis. If you start a social media support option and later abandon it, social media–savvy customers will find out, and they are unforgiving.

Product Innovation

In addition to increased sales, improved customer service, and greater marketing efficiency, online marketing allows companies to get continuous, real-time feedback from current and prospective customers. An entire industry has emerged to help companies better connect with their most influential customers in an effort to perfect and refine their ongoing product development. Companies like Lithium, Jive, and Bazaarvoice have

BE INNOVATIVE

Companies that take time to listen to their clients and make bold and innovative products tend to lead their industries.

redefined the way we connect with customers online, which I talk about soon.

Social media is a great tool for rapid product development. However, there are no secrets online, so be careful of exposing your deep product secrets on the web. There are numerous ways you can use social media to help with product innovation and collaboration.

FOR EXAMPLE

JIVE

Jive Software leads the world as a social business provider—delivering social technology innovations from the consumer world to enterprises securely and at scale, altering how work is completed. The platform blends the power of big data, enterprise integrations, and social collaboration technologies. Millions of people at large organizations use Jive-powered networks internally and externally to break through barriers and change the way they do business. Across diverse industries, these companies are achieving breakthrough results in employee collaboration, customer service, and marketing and sales.

New Product Launch

Recently I worked with an advertising agency that represented a company that built motorized surfboards. Since the idea of powered surfboards was a radically new approach to traditional surfing, the company wanted to do some product testing before spending a ton of money bringing the new surfboard to market. The company leveraged social media to gain immediate feedback on how the new product would be perceived by surfers and what the proposed pricing should be. To accomplish this, the agency first identified existing websites, bloggers, and groups that focused on traditional surfing. With permission from the website owners, the company posted a demonstration video on these sites followed by a survey. It posed questions such as: Would you buy this product? How much would you pay for it? Where would you expect to purchase it? The type of feedback these questions produced was invaluable to

> **BUILDING ONLINE COMMUNITIES**
>
> 
>
>
> An online community is a website wherein people gather in a virtual sense to share opinions, experiences, and ideas, with the aim of helping one another. This can be done through message boards, blogs, or article postings. Many successful companies have built virtual stores around their online communities—targeting the products in their stores to the needs of their community members.

the surfboard company and helped it make better product decisions before the launch.

Community Support

Platforms like Lithium (lithium.com) help companies build entire communities around products and services. Similar to a forum, these communities reduce the major expense of customer support by opening a public forum for customers to answer each others' questions. The company collects these questions and uses them for product improvements and additional product training. The continuous loop of information gives companies an instant view on how customers perceive their products.

Product Ratings and Reviews

Bazaarvoice (www.bazaarvoice.com) is a platform that focuses on providing companies with a ratings and review system. I'm sure that you've seen ratings on sites like Amazon.com or Apple. It's popular now to be completely transparent with your product reviews on your own website. Formerly, several companies I worked with were reluctant to place a rating system on their website. Today, however, it's common practice to show your product reviews to potential customers. My advice to companies concerned with product reviews is to do it anyway. Customers are already talking about your products with friends offline and on other social sites. At least by bringing the conversation to your site, you have a chance to refine your products or respond directly to customers regarding their views of your products.

The benefits of online marketing are multiple, and you will learn more of them as you read this book. Online marketing can help you take your business from a small shop to a global enterprise—through the power of community and technology.

Manager's Checklist for Chapter 1

- ☑ Run an ROI calculator to determine your offline marketing costs before jumping online.
- ☑ Ask your audience where they are online through an online survey.
- ☑ Only use social media for customer service if you can commit to it on an ongoing basis.
- ☑ Leverage social media for product innovation through surveys and examples.
- ☑ Be transparent with your customers about your product ratings.

Web 1.0: Search Engine Optimization and Marketing

Google loves brands—build one. —Dave Naylor, SEO expert

To understand online marketing, it is first necessary to have a grasp of the early innovators and businesses that were built entirely online. Each new web technology builds on the technology before it. In all my online marketing training classes, I spend ample time educating people about the history of the web by explaining search engine optimization and e-commerce before moving into strategic online marketing tactics. Like learning a foreign language, once you understand the fundamentals of online technology, it's easier to move into current online marketing methods such as social media.

The Pioneers

The web began with search and commerce. Without pioneers/innovators like Yahoo!, Google, eBay, and Amazon, the web would not be where it is today. These companies set up successful online platforms that allowed us to buy anything online and have it shipped to our doorstep. These companies also enabled us to promote our companies, thoughts, and ideas via blogs, networks, and keywords. It was these innovative companies that paved the way for a variety of successful online ventures.

In this chapter, we first look at the history of a few of these early web companies that set the stage for how online marketing operates today.

Seek Organic Traffic

We have mentioned the word *organic* in relation to online marketing. You might be thinking of hormone-free dairy products, or pesticide-free vegetables. For the purposes of SEO, organic refers to the traffic that comes to a website through natural means—meaning through optimization of keywords on the website—but not through sponsored search engine campaigns to generate clicks from those keywords. Savvy web marketers seek organic traffic to their sites—even if they initially have to pay for sponsored placement to get it started.

Next we examine how each of these companies' technologies functions and how to leverage those technologies for your own marketing uses. Finally, we talk about the evolution of each company and what the future might look like as you become more deeply involved with each of them.

Yahoo!

Before Google, there was Yahoo! and it was wonderful. Yahoo! was not the first technology that provided information online via search. Both America Online and Netscape were way ahead of their time. But for purposes of this book, we stick to tools that are readily available to you today—including those that help you gain an understanding of Yahoo!

Yahoo! was founded in January 1994 by Jerry Yang and David Filo. The company began with a simple information website titled Jerry and David's Guide to the World Wide web. In April 1994, David and Jerry's Guide to the World Wide Web was renamed Yahoo! Within a few short years, Yahoo! dominated the web.

Back in 1996 when I attended Ohio University, Yahoo! was the only search engine available to students on the one library computer capable of connecting to the Internet through a dial-up modem. It only took me a couple of searches for topics that interested me to discover the power of obtaining information online. Everything—the world—was at my fingertips.

Back then, Yahoo! primarily focused on helping Internet users find information via online search. Today, however, it operates as a digital media company that delivers personalized digital content and experiences to web visitors across the globe. Most of Yahoo!'s revenue comes

> **DESCRIPTIVE PAGE TITLES**
>
> MISTAKE PROOFING
>
> Yahoo! places greater weight on on-the-page content than a search engine like Google. While Google is the leading search engine, Yahoo! is the leading content provider/destination. Because Yahoo! is the number one content destination site on the web, Yahoo! references much of its own content in its search results. Be sure to use descriptive page titles and page content on your web pages so they show up higher on Yahoo! results lists. For example, instead of naming your HTML web page something like car1.html, try instead fordescape.html. These root page names typically show up in searches more easily when your site is "crawled" by the search engines.

from advertising, so it's important that you know how Yahoo! works and how you can leverage its platform to acquire customers.

Overture Keyword Selector Tool shows the prior month's search volumes across Yahoo! and its search network (inventory.overture.com).

I've seen newer websites appear faster in the Yahoo! search engine than in other platforms. Getting website visitors is about maximizing all your available options. Use Yahoo! as one of your inbound marketing strategies by leveraging the sources I've described above.

> KEY TERM
>
> **Site crawling** Search engines, such as Google, Yahoo!, and Bing have automated systems that continuously check your website pages for new content and relevant information to display to people searching the web. This automated process is called *crawling*, since the technology "crawls" through your pages looking for new information.

> **USING BACKLINKS**
>
> 
>
>
> Backlinks are important in studying the effectiveness of online marketing. They tell you how your visitors are finding your website.

Google

In January 1996, shortly after Yahoo!, Google began as a research project by Larry Page and Sergey Brin when they were both PhD students at Stanford University. Google was different from Yahoo! It ranked search results by counting how many times the search terms appeared on the page. They called their technology PageRank. This new search technology cat-

Helpful Links

- Use Yahoo! Site Explorer to see how well your website is indexing and which links are appearing (siteexplorer.search .yahoo.com). This is a tool used to ensure that websites continue to get high quality organic search traffic from Bing and Yahoo.
- Overture View Bids Tool displays the top ads and bid prices by keyword in the Yahoo! Search Marketing ad network (uv.bidtool.overture .com/d/search/tools/bid tool).
- Yahoo! Site Explorer shows which pages Yahoo! has indexed from a site and which pages it knows of that link to pages on your site (siteexplorer .search.yahoo.com).
- Yahoo! Mindset shows you how Yahoo! can bias search results more toward informational or commercial search results (mindset.research .yahoo.com).
- Yahoo! Advanced Search Page (search.yahoo.com/web/advanced) makes it easy to look for .edu and .gov backlinks, meaning the hyperlinks link to individual pages on a website or to a website domain (main page):
  - While doing link: www.site.com/page.html searches (links to an individual page).
  - While doing linkdomain: www.site.com/ searches (links to any page on a particular domain).
- Yahoo! Buzz shows the current most popular searches (buzz.yahoo.com).

KEY TERM

Backlinks Website links that take you back to a previous post, article, or story on the website. For example, I write a blog entry that you find interesting. You then go to your own blog and write a post about my blog entry, linking back to my original post. Now your site *backlinks* to my site with a description of the link (anchor text, which we discuss later) that signals to search engines that my site contains quality content.

egorized a website's relevance by the number of pages and the importance of those pages that linked back to the original site. In other words, links from pages that had a higher number of visits held more leverage in increasing search engine rank than links from pages with few visits.

This made the search returns more relevant for the web user looking for information online, and it also made marketers step up their game not only in providing relevant content, but also in trying to ensure that it would attract widespread and ongoing attention.

TRICKS OF THE TRADE

Use Inbound Marketing

Inbound marketing is a term coined by Brian Halligan, CEO and co-founder of HubSpot, an Internet marketing company, and senior lecturer at MIT. His book, *Inbound Marketing: Get Found Using Google, Social Media, and Blog,* also discusses inbound marketing—which is the act of building a web presence that attracts customers to its valuable content. This is a different concept than traditional outbound marketing—such as placing a print advertisement—in that it involves building a base of content internally and helping customers to find it, rather than blasting customers externally and hoping they respond.

Page and Brin originally nicknamed their new search engine BackRub, because the system checked backlinks to estimate a site's importance. Eventually they changed the name to Google, which originated from a misspelling of the word *googol.* A googol is the number 1 followed by one hundred 0s, which was picked to signify that the search engine wants to provide large quantities of information for people.

CAUTION

Don't Ignore the Popularity Game

It is not enough to have compelling content. That content also must be read or linked to sites that are read in order to receive priority ranking by Google. Google ranks pages partially on their importance. Think of this as ranking the site's popularity—that is, how many times its pages are accessed. It pays to be popular on the web!

Even though the focus of this chapter is largely about SEO (search engine optimization) and SEM (search engine marketing), I include two other pioneers who have led the way in e-commerce. Both eBay and Amazon.com exploded on the web scene at the same time that Yahoo! and Google were emerging. Since this book is about web marketing, you should understand how valuable these shopping web platforms have become in helping companies grow their business. Both Amazon and eBay have grown so large that they now allow advertising directly in their web communities without having to sell your products through them. Maneuverability is key when it comes to online marketing, and these shopping platforms provide tremendous rewards when combined with your SEO and SEM efforts.

KEY TERM

Google AdWords A tool on Google that lets you set up PPC (pay-per-click) campaigns on specific keywords—bidding based on the specific ranking build and analyzing the results in real time. Placing an ad with Google AdWords allows your site to appear in the sponsored category within Google search results. The price paid for each click depends on the competition for the specific keyword.

The tool can also be used to conduct free research of specific keywords and their popularity and to build your own organic inbound marketing campaign through SEO.

Helpful Search Engine Links

TOOLS

Here are some links associated with Google designed to help you use this search engine in your marketing efforts.

- **Google Sitemaps** helps you determine if Google is having problems indexing your site (google.com/webmasters/sitemaps).
- **AdWords Keyword Tool** allows you to enter a keyword, web page, or website and receive recommendations for other keywords to use (adwords.google.com/select/KeywordToolExternal). This tool helps you find the best specific keywords to target on your website (which we discuss later)—and to show you how much competition you will have if you try to capitalize on those keywords.
- **AdWords Traffic Estimator** estimates the PPC bid price required to rank number one on 85 percent of Google AdWords ads that appear near Google search results, and how much traffic an AdWords ad would bring to your site (adwords.google.com/select/TrafficEstimatorSandbox).
- **Google Suggest** automatically completes search queries based on the most common prior searches that begin with the characters or words you have entered so far (google.com/webhp?complete=1&hl=en).
- **Google Trends** shows multiyear search trends (google.com/trends).
- **Google Zeitgeist** shows trends and patterns in web searches—including quickly rising and falling search queries (google.com/press/zeitgeist.html).
- **Google Related Sites** shows sites that Google thinks are related to your site.
- **Google Related Word Search** shows terms semantically related to a keyword term (google.com/search?q=%7Eseo+-seo).

eBay

> **Maneuverability** The ability to change course and adjust a marketing campaign quickly. Think about a sports car that can maneuver around corners and turn on a dime versus a semi truck that would take ages to get up to speed, turn corners, and stop. Online marketing offers maneuverability in that it can be turned on or off—or changed—quickly.
>
> KEY TERM

In 1995 in San Jose, California, Pierre Omidyar founded eBay, then called AuctionWeb. According to Adam Cohen's 2002 book, *The Perfect Store,* one of the first items sold on eBay was a broken laser pointer for $14.83. Surprised, Omidyar apparently contacted the winning bidder to ask if he knew that the laser pointer was broken. The buyer responded: "I'm a collector of broken laser pointers."

In 1997, the company officially changed its name from AuctionWeb to eBay. Originally, the site belonged to Echo Bay Technology Group, Omidyar's consulting firm. Omidyar had tried to register the domain name echobay.com, but found it already taken by a gold mining company, so he shortened it to his second choice, eBay.com.

Helpful eBay Links

TOOLS

These two links will guide you in using eBay for your online selling efforts:

- **eBay Selling Tools** helps you list items on eBay and track results (pages.ebay.com/sellerinformation/sellingresources/sellingtools.html).
- **eBay Advertising** lets you advertise your products or services with the eBay community without needing to sell your product on eBay (ebayadvertising.com/en-us).

Amazon.com

In 1995 Jeff Bezos founded Amazon, which began as an online bookstore. I vividly recall investors and the media talking about Amazon back in 1997. There was a ton of resistance when it came to launching Internet-based companies, especially a bookstore. Several media sources had predicted that Amazon would fail. At this writing, Jeff Bezos is one of the wealthiest people in the world, with a net worth of more than $18 billion, according to *Forbes*.

Helpful Amazon Links

Here are some links to help you use Amazon.com in your marketing and selling program:

- **Amazon Webstore** lets you set up your own store and customize it using easy editing tools (webstore.amazon.com).
- **Amazon Fulfillment** lets you store your products in Amazon's fulfillment centers, and Amazon directly packs, ships, and provides customer service for these products (amazonservices.com/content/fulfillment-by-amazon.htm).
- **Checkout by Amazon** is a complete checkout and payments service for e-commerce retailers. Offering Checkout by Amazon enables millions of Amazon customers to use shipping addresses and payment information in their Amazon.com accounts to buy from your e-commerce or mobile website. Customers complete purchases quickly and conveniently, without ever leaving your website (amazonservices .com/content/amazon-checkout-payments.htm).
- **Amazon Product Ads** advertises your products and drives traffic to your website from Amazon.com (amazonservices.com/content/product-ads-on-amazon.htm).
- **Amazon Display Ads** reaches a broad audience using precise targeting capabilities (amazonservices.com/content/amazon-display-advertising.htm).

Traffic Alone Isn't Enough

"Trying to increase sales simply by driving more traffic to a website with a poor customer conversion rate is like trying to keep a leaky bucket full by adding more water instead of plugging the holes." —Bryan Eisenberg and Jeffrey Eisenberg, coauthors, *Call to Action*

There are several ways to leverage Amazon to get more business. From listing your products on the Amazon.com site to using its commerce tools on your own site to display or advertise products, we explore the ways you can position your products or services. Amazon is now the world's largest online marketplace, selling everything from computers to clothes, and yes, even books.

Now that we have identified the pioneers in the early days of the web, let's look at how you can leverage each of these technologies to promote your products or services online. It's time to roll up our sleeves and get to work on strategies around these platforms. Let's begin!

Search Engine Optimization

To master SEO (search engine optimization), you need to understand how each platform (Yahoo!, Google, Bing) works. Every search platform is based on a series of mathematical algorithms that determine where your search return should appear in the search results rankings. Each platform approaches a search differently.

> **CHANGES TO SEARCH ENGINES**
>
> CAUTION
>
> Before we explore how to get the most from these search engines, it's important to understand that algorithms continuously evolve. Companies like Bing, Yahoo!, and Google are always looking for ways to improve their technology. Use the practices in this book, but also study each platform at least once a year to make sure you are following its technical procedures for the best search returns. For example, Google's search technology evolution can be found at techi.com/2012/03/googles-search-algorithm-changes-1998-2012. This information graphic should show how frequently Google has updated its search engine since 1998.

Here's more on these major search engines:

Yahoo!

- Yahoo! uses its web directory as part of its ranking algorithm. If you have a business website on Yahoo!, you must pay $299 annually to appear and remain in the Yahoo Web Directory. For organizations or informational websites, you can try to "suggest a site" (dir.yahoo.com).
- Make certain that the name of your website contains your major keywords. The website's title is the most important ranking factor in Yahoo!'s algorithm.
- Click popularity is part of Yahoo!'s algorithm, meaning the more visitors who click on your website from Yahoo! SERP (search engine results page), the closer you'll get to the top ranking.
- The category in which you

> **SEARCH ENGINE REGISTRATION**
>
> CAUTION
>
> Do not submit all your web pages to Yahoo!; you only need to submit your home page. Yahoo! views submission of all your pages as spamming. That can result in banning your website from the search engine, and you might never appear on Yahoo!

are listed in the Yahoo Web Directory should contain some of your targeted or desired keywords.
- Separate from submitting to the Yahoo! Directory, you must also submit it to Yahoo!'s search engine (go to search.yahoo.com/info/submit.html).

Google

No search engine strategy is complete without gaining an understanding of how Google ranks its pages and how to use that understanding to your advantage. Consider these facts about Google:

- Google is better than the other search engines at determining if a link is a true editorial citation or an artificial link.
- Google heavily biases search results toward resources that contain informational content that continuously changes, which is why blogs rank well on Google's SERP.
- Older websites and subdomains typically rank higher than newer sites.
- Google has an aggressive duplicate content filter. It filters out many pages with similar content. Be careful not to overlap your website with pages that contain duplicate content as it could be filtered out by Google.
- Google's crawl technology is determined not only by link quantity, but also link quality. Low-quality links are likely to affect your search with Google. A *low-quality link* is defined as a link that goes to a page that does not contain very good or very much content and therefore doesn't receive much web traffic.

> **OUTSMARTING GOOGLE?**
>
> CAUTION
>
> In the past, people used to create multiple pages with the same keywords in an attempt to inundate the search engines with content and drive results. Today, Google's algorithms are more complex. You will have stronger long-term results if you use the tips in this chapter to work with—rather than against—Google.

Bing

To understand how Bing works, consider these key points:

- Bing places less emphasis on backlinks than Google.
- Inbound anchor text helps you rank higher on Bing. Create quality anchor text, and you will do well in both Bing and Google. For example,

the hyperlink would look like hondaaccord.html, and the descriptive anchor text would explain the link: honda accord 2012 model.

Anchor text The descriptive labeling of hyperlinks.

- Your pages' content helps with your Bing search ranking more than with Google. Make sure you have quality content on your pages relevant to the people you want to attract.
- Bing pays more attention to the authority or age of a website than Google. This means that search results favor older sites and/or sites of authoritative organizations. Your website's domain age is more important with Bing than with Google.
- Fresh content matters less with Bing than with Google. This means that frequent content updates do not appear to have much of an impact on Bing's search results.
- Bing is more Adobe® Flash–friendly. A Google search typically punishes websites designed using Flash-specific key terms. However, Bing appears to have an effective way to crawl Flash sites.

FLASH

The web is becoming more mobile phone–friendly. Websites that use Flash are not viewable on several mobile phones. Additionally, Google does not crawl Flash sites well. Adobe® recently announced that it would stop developing tools to support Flash websites. Therefore, I do not recommend building a new website using Flash.

Amazon

Even though Amazon is an e-commerce platform, it has built its own proprietary search and product recommendation engine. Amazon's search calculation is based on hourly updated sales figures. Amazon's product descriptions use key phrases to direct shoppers to your items.

Product rankings are based on sales figures calculated by considering the current ranking of the item and how many items have been sold compared to your competitors. For example, a book that has sold 700 copies in the last hour will receive a higher ranking than a book that has sold 100 copies. Here are some tips for getting the most from your Amazon marketing:

- Use search terms for every product you post on Amazon.
- Make sure your product names actually describe your product. For example, use "men's blue wool socks" instead of merely "socks."
- Do not use quotation marks or bullets in search terms. Punctuation will not appear in Amazon's search, and thus, an item will not show up if you have listed it using punctuation.
- Use alternative spellings in your key terms. For example, American English would spell *organize* and British English would spell *organise*. Use both in your key terms.
- Don't use abbreviations. People search for the full product name.

You don't need to populate your key terms with misspellings of your products. Amazon's powerful search engine compensates for common customer misspellings and offers corrective suggestions.

eBay

eBay has a powerful e-commerce platform with its own search tools. Both Amazon and eBay products tie into Google's platform when searching for products on Google. Therefore, it's important to accurately position your products on eBay so they have a better chance of being found on Google as well.

- The first step in SEO for eBay is to choose effective keywords. To select keywords, think of how your customers would search for your products and what keywords you would enter if you were looking for your products online.
- To improve the search engine ranking of your eBay store, encourage as many others as possible to link their website (external website link) to your eBay store.

Network for Links

TRICKS OF THE TRADE

Encourage your business associates and online friends to link to your eBay store. This helps with your organic search return on eBay.

Categorize Your Listings

TOOLS

eBay makes it easy to categorize your listings. It even provides a tool so you can see a list of all keyword to category mappings. Go to the Keyword-to-Category Mapping help page for assistance (pages.ebay .com/ help/find/search-expansions.html).

- eBay item titles can be up to 55 characters long. Include information that describes key characteristics of the item to help potential customers save time in their eBay search.

TRICKS OF THE TRADE

KEYWORDS

Repeating a keyword in a number of places such as your store URL, item title, and item description will increase eBay's search engine's perception of how relevant your web page is to a particular keyword. Your store name should be descriptive. For example, Apple iPhone Accessories is better than Joe's Cell Phone Shack. Everything from your product titles, descriptions, store name, and eBay user ID (which is displayed whenever you buy or sell on eBay or communicate with other members)—should be reviewed as an opportunity to leverage keywords for optimal search return results.

Making the Most of SEO

Optimizing your website may involve editing its content and HTML to increase its relevance to specific keywords. In the steps below, I explain how to set up your site so you have the fewest barriers to the search engines' indexing activities. Other tactics may include creating your site in a way to increase the number of backlinks (incoming links to your site from sites you have linked to) or inbound links (links to your site from other sites that you don't link back to).

KEY TERM

Indexing "Includes back-of-book-style indexes to individual websites or an intranet, and the creation of keyword metadata to provide a more useful vocabulary for Internet or onsite search engines" (Wikipedia). Indexing uses specific keywords so that the web page or site can be recognized and retrieved by a search engine.

Properly written title tags on a website are critical. Title tags are part of the meta tags that appear at the top of your HTML inside the < head> area. Title tags are also part of what makes people decide whether to visit your site when it shows up in the search results. The title tag should contain important keywords to help the search engine determine what the page is about. A title tag is the most important tag in your page. It tells the search engines what your page is about. Here's a quick checklist with some tips on how to write optimized title tags and improve your SEO strategy:

Optimizing Your Site for Better Search Ranking

Follow these tips to ensure your website is properly optimized for search engine results:

- Make sure your site tells Google that it's OK to crawl. Check your site status by visiting a third-party verification tool such as rexswain.com /httpview.html. You should see a 200 OK code to search engines. This code tells search engines your page is open for crawling (scanning your site for relevant content). You can read about all the HTTP status codes on Wikipedia (en.wikipedia.org/wiki/List_of_HTTP_ status_codes).
- Limit use of JavaScript code for your website navigation. JavaScript is not as crawlable as traditional HTML.
- Don't build an Adobe Flash website. Flash-based websites are virtually invisible to search engines. Text contained in Flash is not searchable by Google or other platforms.
- Avoid having too much code on your site. Move JavaScript or CSS code to external files and ensure your most important text is toward the top of your HTML code.
- Avoid displaying multiple pages with the same content, as Google filters out all duplicates from its search results. If you have more than one page with the same text, change it so every page has different text.

- Write a descriptive <TITLE> tag for each page. This title tag is the HTML code area that describes your web page's title.
- Include the name of the actual page file (in most cases this is your HTML document). Instead of naming your file products.html, use the more descriptive blue-socks-men.html.
- Each page should have an <H1> heading. Headings are like subtitles on a page that break up the text into topics. Think of a heading as similar to beginning a new paragraph. Headings should describe the text on your page.
- Since most search engines cannot index images, it's important to include descriptive text on any page you want to appear in Google, Yahoo!, or Bing SERP. Be sure to add <ALT> tags to each image. ALT tags are text descriptions in your code for each image. These tags also help users who are visually impaired find what they need on your site using an audio reader.
- Each link to your site from another site is an opportunity to rank higher in Google's search results. Try to get links from your external

website partners, bloggers, and the media to help with your external link strategy. Make sure they use descriptive anchor text to achieve maximum results.

Meta tags HTML codes inserted into the header on a web page after the title tag. In the context of SEO, when people refer to meta tags, they usually mean the meta description tag and the meta keywords tag. Users do not see the meta description tag. The purpose of these tags is to provide meta document data (meta elements) for search engines.

Meta elements HTML or XHTML elements that provide information about a web page for the search engines and website users. Such elements must be placed as tags in the head section of an HTML document. These elements are the:

- title tag
- description
- keywords

Keywords Typically one-word descriptions used to describe a link, an object or a product online. For example, keywords to describe this book may include *web, marketing, SEO.*

Key phrases Similar to keywords, but key phrases are typically short sentences that describe a link, object, or online product. For example, a key phrase for this book might be *managers guide to web marketing.*

Relevance In the context of search engines, this means how accurately the information provided by a website matches the information requested by a person searching for information. The higher the relevance, the more likely the information on your site will be found.

Domain The public website name used in place of an IP address. The IP address is the numerical address associated with a device on a network—such as a computer. Your domain is normally the registered name of your website, and is typically much easier to remember than an IP address. For example, my company has a website with domain name of shoutlet.com.

Search Engine Marketing, aka Pay-per-Click

I'm sure you've heard the expression "You get what you pay for." The same is true for online marketing. For years, online marketing professionals have been trying to optimize their websites to appear higher in organic searches. Unfortunately, nothing in this world is free. Google, Yahoo!, and Bing all make money from advertising. The only way to guarantee qualified web visitors to your website is by spending money with one of these companies.

Many of these sites have training and certification programs to help you learn the art of search engine marketing (SEM, paid placement of your website within the search engine results). These businesses know that the more money you make using their tools, the more you'll spend with them. The good news is that many of the same practices you learned about SEO keywords, search terms, and relevancy also apply to SEM.

There are several options for advertising on these platforms, but there are two primary types of advertising: keyword and display.

1. **Keyword advertising** (known as AdWords on Google) is the most common type of advertising because it does not require artwork, as it's based on search words and descriptions alone. Keyword ads appear on the top or in a sidebar on Google when you search for a key term.
2. **Display ads** (sometimes known as banner ads) are more graphic in appearance and are designed like a billboard on your local highway. Although they may appear to be more visually appealing than keyword ads, they are less likely to appear in search results since images, videos, and Flash assets are not crawlable like keywords.

I have seen most companies use keyword advertising effectively in driving traffic to their sites. Display advertising works well if you are advertising a relevant product or service on a targeted website. For example, you would advertise your famous BBQ sauce on a website focused on grilling and BBQ lovers.

I recommend beginning with keyword advertising and trying display ads later, once you have a feel for your *conversion rate* (the rate at which you convert website visitors to sales). Since search companies have made it easy for you to learn how to advertise on their sites, I recommend you visit each one and test some small ads before you launch a full-scale online campaign.

TOOLS

KEYWORDS

Use third-party tools to research which keywords your potential customers are using. You can find a simple, free tool here: www.keyworddiscovery.com/search.html.

ADVERTISING OPTIONS

TOOLS

Below are options for advertising based on keywords or display ads:

- **Google AdWords.** To advertise your keywords on Google, go to adwords.google.com.
- **AdWords Certification.** To get certified in Google AdWords (online training), go to google.com/adwords/professionals.
- **Yahoo! Advertising Solutions.** To advertise on Yahoo!, go to advertising.yahoo.com.
- **Amazon Product Ads.** To advertise your products and drive traffic to your website from Amazon.com, go to amazonservices.com/content /product-ads-on-amazon.htm.
- **Amazon Display Ads.** To reach a broad audience using precise targeting, go to amazonservices.com/content/amazon-display-advertising.htm.
- **eBay Advertising.** Advertise your products or services to the eBay community without having to sell your product on eBay. Go to ebayadvertising.com/en-us.

Many other online advertising options exist, such as with large content-based websites like magazines or newspapers. Inquire with advertising directors or site managers to determine advertising rates, and before you commit to placing an ad, be sure you understand and analyze the number of impressions or clicks you are being offered.

The trick with SEM is knowing what people search for when trying to find your products or services online. SEM specialists (a person or a company that offers SEO services) have an artful way to test keywords.

Google has an effective keyword tool to help you determine which words will be most effective to use in your advertising (https:// adwords.google.com). Google also tells you the potential traffic you can expect for each keyword.

SEM is an ongoing job. Many companies have hired full-time staff to run their SEM/SEO efforts. Several consultants and agencies are also available to help with your search and advertising needs. However, you can get started without hiring outside help. Google makes it easy to advertise, but maintaining a campaign and optimizing its effectiveness can easily turn into a full-time job.

Once you've begun the process of sending visitors to your website, you'll soon discover that you want to create forced actions so these visitors either buy your product or fill out a form with their information. Several SEO/SEM experts use landing pages for that purpose.

Landing Pages

A *landing page* is sometimes known as a *lead capture page*. These pages are designed to be a single web page that appears in response to clicking on a keyword or display ad from a search engine site. A landing page usually displays sales information about a specific product or service and limits the visitor's options to navigating away from the page.

BE RELEVANT Make sure your landing pages contain content relevant to the visitor. Don't make your page an advertisement; strive to make it informational. Include keywords in your HTML that appear in SERPs.

Landing pages are *SEO optimized*, meaning they contain keywords that help the page tie into a SERP. Since the landing page is isolated from the rest of the website, you can easily track the results of an ad campaign based on the amount of website traffic it receives.

Several tools on the market today help create and track landing pages instantly. Tools include platforms from marketing automation companies like Marketo, Aprimo, Eloqua, and HubSpot, to social media page creation tools like Shoutlet. You can see great examples of landing pages by visiting any of these websites.

Just as landing pages help with SEO and SEM, affiliate marketing programs help with e-commerce and getting your products sold directly through commission-based *evangelists*, a concept we discuss later in this book.

Affiliate Marketing Programs

Affiliate marketing is a practice in which a business rewards one or more affiliates for each visitor or customer brought about by the affiliate's own marketing efforts.

KEY TERM

Affiliate A site that sells a product or service on your behalf, typically earning a commission for sales generated. Affiliate income is typically tracked through unique links provided by third-party management sites, or a robust internal tracking system, such as in companies like Amazon.

Affiliate marketing exploded onto the scene when Amazon launched a way for its customers to sell books on their own websites and blogs in exchange for a commission.

Affiliate marketing has been widely popularized over the past decade, producing several variations of affiliate marketing platforms and programs for web customers to make affiliate revenue.

While sites like eBay and Amazon have built their own affiliate networks, several third-party providers have also been launched to help companies reach affiliates across the entire web. Services like Commission Junction and Linkshare dominate the external affiliate network platforms. Amazon still has an incredible affiliate program (affiliate-program.amazon.com), too.

SMART MANAGING

Affiliate Marketing Platforms Are Like Toll Booths

Think of affiliate marketing platforms like toll booths on a busy highway. When cars leave one section of road, they must pay a toll that allows them to continue. The toll goes to a government or third-party management organization to maintain that section of the road. Similarly, an affiliate platform allows web visitors to leave your site and purchase products from another site—while leaving a toll that goes to you for maintaining that "road" or link.

Affiliate Marketing Checklist

Here is a checklist for running an affiliate marketing program.

- ❑ **Know your audience.** Make sure you create the right affiliate program for the right audience. I have seen several affiliate programs run campaigns on sites that have zero to do with the campaign content. For example, if you are running an affiliate program to sell laptop cases, make sure your affiliate program runs on computer sites, not automobile sites.
- ❑ **Pay enough of an incentive to get them going.** Make sure your commission or incentive to sell your product is enough for the affiliate to really care about promoting it. I've seen companies too cheap to make any real impact with their affiliate marketing. You can always reduce the commission later if you feel it's too much, but realize that getting some revenue for very little effort is better than getting none.
- ❑ **Do the work for the affiliates.** Develop compelling content in the form of text descriptions, videos, or display ads so that your affiliates can market your products easily.
- ❑ **Be transparent.** Make yourself accessible and open for communication. web visitors get suspicious if you fail to provide company contact information or product shipping and return details, etc.

Affiliate network platforms connect the product/service providers with the buyers and users.

Finally, if you only have one product to sell, you can use Spendship .com to market it to your close circle of friends—allowing them to earn commissions for sales they generate through their unique links.

Successful online marketing starts by gaining an understanding of prominent search engines—such as Yahoo! and Google—and how they drive traffic today. Your online marketing success also depends on gaining a basic understanding of the tools available to you, including SEO and affiliate marketing—and platforms like eBay and Amazon. Now that you've gained this understanding, you're ready to move on to social media!

TRICKS OF THE TRADE

Being Smart About the Menace of Spam

Monitor the web frequently for how your company is being represented through your affiliate networks. It's easy to find people on affiliate networks who will pick up your program and spam the entire web in hopes of making quick revenue—e-mailing an offer for your products indiscriminately to anyone and everyone they can find with an e-mail address. This is the primary reason you see so much Viagra and home refinancing garbage online. Many of these companies pay high commissions, so the veteran affiliates spam the web until they are shut down. Setting up an automated Google search (Google Alerts) that e-mails you when your company is mentioned should help you keep track of potential issues (google.com/alerts).

Manager's Checklist for Chapter 2

- ☑ SEO (search engine optimization) and SEM (search engine marketing) are the fundamental technologies for running marketing programs.
- ☑ SEO is the art of creating and maintaining how high and how frequently you appear in a SERP (search engine results page).
- ☑ SEM is paid advertising by using purchased keywords.
- ☑ Landing pages guide website visitors to a predetermined action (purchase a product, fill out a form) and can yield better SEO results and tracking.
- ☑ Affiliate programs enable people to sell your products or services online for a commission.

Social Media (Web 2.0)

You are what you tweet. —Alex Tew, *Monkey Inferno*

Social media has exploded in the last few years. Every company leader I speak with today wants to know how he or she can leverage social media to gain more fans, followers, and ultimately, customers. Much like the previous chapter, it's important to know the history of each social platform today before you can fully grasp how to use it for your company's marketing efforts. By comparison with Web 1.0, social media has the power to make conversations or content take off like wildfire. A story or video that gets mentioned once on a small website or blog can have millions of viewers or readers within hours.

In this chapter, we discuss the history of today's most powerful social networks, how they operate, and how to leverage these networks to promote your products, services, or company's image. We also explore mobile pages and applications that support these networks by driving on-the-go visitors to these networks.

The Pioneers

You may remember social platforms such as MySpace and Friendster. Social networks quickly come and go on the web. That's why it's important to stay maneuverable, meaning always having a diverse mix of marketing strategies across several social networks. Even though there were

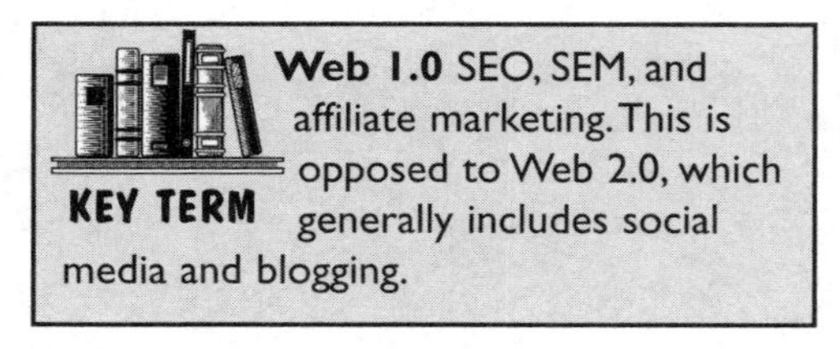

several social platforms before Facebook, Twitter, and YouTube, we focus on today's core social media platforms since they are the most popular now and because they have proven to be successful in helping brands market online.

KEY TERM
Web 1.0 SEO, SEM, and affiliate marketing. This is opposed to Web 2.0, which generally includes social media and blogging.

Facebook

Mark Zuckerberg wrote Facemash, the predecessor to Facebook, in 2003 while a sophomore at Harvard. According to *The Harvard Crimson*, the site was comparable to Hot or Not, and "used photos compiled from the online facebooks of nine houses, placing two next to each other at a time and asking users to choose the 'hotter' person" (Katherine Kaplan, "Facebook Creator Survives Ad Board," *The Harvard Crimson*, November 19, 2003). The Facebook was incorporated in mid-2004, and the entrepreneur Sean Parker, who had been informally advising Zuckerberg, became the company's president. In June 2004, The Facebook moved its base of operations to Palo Alto, California. It received its first investment later that month from PayPal cofounder Peter Thiel. The company dropped *The* from its name after purchasing the domain name facebook.com in 2005 for $200,000.

At this writing, Facebook is the world's largest website with more than 900 million users worldwide.

Twitter

Twitter is an online social networking service and microblogging service that enables its users to send and read text-based posts of up to 140 characters, known as *tweets*.

Twitter was created in 2006 by Jack Dorsey and launched that same year. The service rapidly gained worldwide popularity, with more than 140 million active users as of 2012, generating more than 340 million tweets daily and handling more than 1.6 billion search queries per day. It has been described as "the SMS of the Internet." Unregistered users can read the tweets, while registered users can post tweets through the website interface, SMS, or a range of apps for mobile devices. The Twitter website is one of the top 10 most visited on the Internet.

YouTube

YouTube is a video-sharing website on which users can upload, view, and share videos.

YouTube was founded by Chad Hurley, Steve Chen, and Jawed Karim, who were early PayPal employees. Hurley had studied design at Indiana University of Pennsylvania, while Chen and Karim studied computer science together at the University of Illinois at Urbana-Champaign.

TWEETS VS. STATUS UPDATES — SMART MANAGING

Tweets originated with Twitter—and often include a short description of what someone is doing or thinking—or sometimes a few words of value. In Facebook (discussed shortly), these updates are called *status updates*. Both offer a way to engage customers, friends, and fans with news and ideas.

YouTube began as a venture-funded technology start-up, primarily from an $11.5 million investment by Sequoia Capital between November 2005 and April 2006. YouTube's early headquarters were situated above a pizzeria and Japanese restaurant in San Mateo, California. The domain name youtube.com was activated on February 14, 2005, and the website was developed over the subsequent months.

In 2006, Google Inc. announced that it had acquired YouTube for $1.65 billion in Google stock.

Google+

Google+ (pronounced Google Plus) launched its social network to the public in September 2011. Google+ integrates social services such as Google Profiles, Circles, Hangouts, and Sparks. Google+ is available as a website and on mobile devices. Sources such as the *New York Times* have declared it Google's biggest attempt to rival Facebook.

KEY TERM

Google+ A relatively new social network by Google. Google's platform has some subtle differences for brand marketers that make it easy to find your company online. Keep in mind that Google still leads searches in terms of the most usage, so it has an advantage over Facebook in driving web traffic.

Google's advantage over Facebook is its integration into its other services, such as Gmail and YouTube. According to a December 2011 independent analysis of Google+'s growth, the site was adding an estimated 625,000 users each day, which could total 400 million members by the end of 2012.

Social Media Marketing Strategies

Facebook

Similar to Yahoo!, Google, and Bing, which we discussed in the previous chapter, *EdgeRank* is an algorithm developed by Facebook to govern what content from users is displayed and how high it appears on the news feed.

In Facebook, the news feed is similar to the search engine results page (SERP) from Yahoo!, Google, or Bing. However, in Facebook, the news feed content is created by your own *friends* instead of information gathered from across the web.

KEY TERM

News feed The center column of your home page that is a constantly refreshing list of real-time updates from people and pages that you have linked with on Facebook.

Understanding how to improve your EdgeRank on Facebook is the key to creating more interaction with your Facebook fans.

Facebook's algorithm can be understood as the sum of edges. Each edge is made up of a few key areas that include affinity, weight, and time

SMART MANAGING

THE DIFFERENCE BETWEEN FACEBOOK FRIENDS AND FANS

A Facebook *friend* is a user accepted into another person's network, allowing him or her to access the friend's profile. A personal *profile* is the account that a user maintains, consisting of information about the user. Users may post information about their work, relationship status, family members, education, hobbies—as well as photos and updates about what they are doing or thinking. They may also share information with their friends list.

Facebook users are connected as friends by sending Facebook *friend requests* to others—who become friends when the invitation is accepted (the invitation may also be denied).

A Facebook *fan* is a user who has "liked" a business or brand page. We detail these pages and how to acquire fans later in this chapter.

Profiles and pages may also be published in the newer Timeline format, categorizing information in tabs by year.

decay. Here is more detail on these concepts:

> **Facebook news feed** The real time scrolling of updates from your Facebook friends—including indications of their activities on Facebook, as well as new posts they submit or share.
>
> KEY TERM

Edges are any user action on Facebook. Edges can be status updates, comments, likes, and shares. EdgeRank ranks edges in the news feed. EdgeRank looks at all the edges connected to the user; it then ranks each edge to understand the importance to the user viewing the news feed. Objects with the highest EdgeRank typically go to the top of the news feed.

Affinity is a relationship between a user and an edge. It is the measurement of the "relationship" between a brand and a fan. Affinity is built by repeat interactions with a brand's edges. Actions such as commenting, liking, sharing, clicking, and even messaging influence a user's affinity.

Weight is a value system created by Facebook to increase or decrease the value of certain Facebook actions. A comment is more involved and therefore deemed more valuable than a like.

Time decay refers to how long the edge has been alive; the older it is the less valuable it is. If you are using Facebook today, you are probably already aware of how quickly a post on your news feed disappears. Facebook does this in an effort to keep information fresh and relevant so that every user is continuously engaged.

If your brand has a lower EdgeRank, then fewer people are seeing your content. Since the company I work for is a Preferred Facebook Developer Consultant, I can tell you that I've seen firsthand that brands that create compelling content receive more engagement and, ultimately, a higher EdgeRank.

> **ENCOURAGE INTERACTION**
>
> TRICKS OF THE TRADE
>
> To achieve a higher EdgeRank on Facebook, make sure that you encourage interaction with the content you post on your news feed or timeline. For example, Four Seasons Hotel frequently posts photos of their luxury vacation spots on Facebook with a call to action, "Like, if you wish you were here." Obviously, they receive an extremely high engagement rate because most of us are sitting in an office when we see their beautiful beach resort photos. Posting such no-brainer requests for feedback is a good way to engage fans to become active on your page—thereby increasing your EdgeRank.

Establishing Your Facebook Presence

Now that we've discussed the fundamentals of Facebook, let's discuss how to use it in promoting your business. Here are options for increasing your exposure through Facebook:

Create a page for your business or brand. A Facebook *brand page* allows you to promote your business to Facebook users across their social network (facebook.com/about/pages). Brand pages differ from a *personal profile* (your individual Facebook account), although both may now be published in a *Timeline* format. Listed below are the primary limitations of a brand page.

- Businesses are only allowed to open pages, *not* a profile. A business that opens a profile page is in direct violation of Facebook's Terms of Service (TOS).

> TRICKS OF THE TRADE
>
> **ASSIGNING A USERNAME**
>
> When creating a brand page, you have the option of assigning a username to your page. The username is a unique identity that becomes part of the URL link you give out to potential fans. For example, my company's username on Facebook is shoutlet, which is the name of my company. When promoting my Facebook page, I give out the URL facebook.com/shoutlet.
>
> It's helpful to choose a username that corresponds to your company or branding and is easy to remember, since the username is something you may end up publishing or broadcasting in your marketing materials. Imagine yourself on a radio show giving out your fan page to listeners, and ask yourself, "Is it easy to spell, say, and remember?"
>
> Consider the shelf life of the name you choose, since a username will stick around. Many assign their business name as their username.

- Business pages allow users to become fans of your business, but access to the individuals' profile pages is limited.
- Business pages lack the capability to request friendships—in fact, business pages cannot maintain a friends list, as it is not enabled on business pages. They can only maintain a fan list. They can, however, suggest a business page to those on their personal friends list.
- Business pages do allow the posting of status updates (which get shared with fans).

URL (universal resource locator) An individualized web or social media site address, for example, facebook.com /shoutlet.

Discussion board An area on a page where fans can discuss a subject.

Applications Programs that enhance the usability of a fan page.

Wall posts Items posted to a page by fans.

Groups A place for individuals to connect with like-minded professionals related to your industry in over a million groups. In group discussions, you can share insights, post articles, create polls, and have the group icon on your profile.

- Business pages allow pictures, videos, discussion boards, applications, wall posts, groups, and other interactive elements.
- A business page permits one or several administrators to "ghostwrite" status updates that appear in the timeline. Admins must have a Facebook profile or personal timeline prior to gaining administrative status, but the admin's personal identity is invisible to the fans when the admin posts. The admin can also manage and change settings on the page.

SMART MANAGING

Assigning Facebook Admins

As the creator of a business page, you can assign administrator status to anyone you choose who has a Facebook personal profile or timeline. The advantage to doing this is that you can allow someone to access your business page to post updates without having to log in under your personal profile. Be sure you assign administrator status to someone you trust, since this person can change your page settings at will.

Design a custom app. Facebook *custom apps* (formerly called a tab or page) are customized pages accessible from your *brand page timeline*—a chronology of a brand's life on Facebook. The benefit of having custom apps is that you can develop an entire page with specific page elements for your fans. Additionally, you can create these apps to be *fan-gated*, meaning these apps display content to users who become fans of your brand page. Custom apps also allow you to run contests, insert sign-up forms into your promotions, and even create custom video players (a

FRIEND, FAN, OR FOE?

When building a business page, note that anyone on Facebook can "like" the page—thereby receiving updates in his or her news feed as to your page's activity. Depending on your settings, these same people can post on your page or add comments to your status updates, photos, videos, etc. If you are concerned about the free flow of correspondence or the lack of control over who posts what, you may change your settings to limit others' ability to post on your page. For example, some administrators may be worried about negative posts, or posts from competitors that either bombard users with pitches or encourage them to take their business elsewhere. Most business page administers, however, welcome the exchange in the name of communication and community—and accept its risks.

branded video player offering an alternative to YouTube), etc. Companies that leverage these apps acquire information about their fans (such as e-mail address and interests) because apps are controlled by your company and can be used any way you choose, as long as doing so doesn't violate Facebook's TOS.

SMART MANAGING

USING CUSTOM APPS

Since page admins can no longer designate a default landing tab (also referred to as the default welcome tab), businesses need to become more creative and use custom apps to direct Facebook page visitors to take action. Instead of having apps on the left side of your page, they're now featured directly below the cover photo.

One way to make up for the loss of engagement with a default landing tab is to drive visitors to your custom apps instead.

Fill your business timeline. Recently Facebook introduced timeline (facebook.com/about/timeline), which we touched on earlier. This is nothing more than a chronological list of your company's events and activities, with the most recent at the top of your page, and tabs for each year—making it easy to browse past content. A timeline forces businesses and individuals to talk about their lives or existence in terms of a storyboard. For brands, it's an opportunity to insert a ton of information about your company.

Browse Facebook and take a look at some of the ways companies leverage their timeline.

Add a like button to Your website. The *Like* button is based on Facebook's Open Graph Protocol (developers.connect.facebook.com/docs/reference/plugins/like). This technology enables you to integrate your web pages into Facebook's social graph; that is, when a user clicks a Like button on your page, a connection is made between your page and the user. Your page will appear in the Likes and Interests section of the user's profile, and you then have the ability to publish updates to the user's page. Your page will show up in the search bar, and you can target ads to people who like your content. The structured data—or tags—you provide via the Open Graph Protocol defines how your page will be represented on Facebook.

> **FORD MOTOR COMPANY PAVES THE ROAD**
>
> FOR EXAMPLE
>
> Ford Motor Company does an excellent job of leveraging its timeline. See facebook.com/ford to see how they detail their history as well as their current endeavors.

Run a contest. Once you've created a custom app on your Facebook brand page, you can run contests and promotions. My company, Shoutlet (shoutlet.com), specializes in providing easy ways to create and run Facebook contests. They are a great way to gain fans quickly. People are eager to Like a page if there is a chance to win something. Experiment with contests and use the sign-up portion of your contest as a way to gather additional information about your fans.

> **RUNNING FACEBOOK CONTESTS**
>
> TRICKS OF THE TRADE
>
> Running a contest on Facebook is an excellent way to collect information that may not be gathered from alternate marketing methods such as direct mail, e-mails blasts, etc. For example, if your company were to create a Facebook contest using certain apps, you can collect information around the participants' interests such as what books they read, what TV shows they watch, their favorite vacation spots, etc. By also including a sign-up form in your contest, you get information that Facebook does not provide such as: where is their favorite place to go camping? This targeted information is useful for a variety of direct marketing purposes. For example, I can collect information for a certain zip code and provide targeted marketing campaigns based on demographics, income level etc.

Advertise on Facebook. Just like the search engines (Google, Yahoo!, Bing) mentioned in the previous chapter, Facebook makes its money from advertising (facebook.com/advertising). More weight is given to companies trying to build Facebook fans if they spend money with Facebook than companies that merely have a free brand page. Creating Facebook ads is easy and effective. Once your brand page is established, try some advertising to see if your fan base grows. Remember, compelling content is key to engaging fans.

FOR EXAMPLE

Rayovac Batteries

Rayovac started its Facebook brand page with zero fans. It also wanted to build an e-mail database for direct marketing purposes. Over Thanksgiving weekend (the height of the battery buying season), Rayovac launched a $1 Off coupon in the form of a shareable web app and posted it to coupon sites everywhere. Web visitors would click on the app and enter their e-mail address to receive the coupon. The app could also be shared on Facebook. Within five days, Rayovac had collected more than 5,000 e-mail addresses and new Facebook fans. Rayovac leveraged external websites (coupon networks) to drive fans to its Facebook page, which achieved the desired results.

Facebook Tools

TOOLS

- Check your EdgeRank using tools like EdgeRank Checker (edgerankchecker.com).
- Facebook Insights (facebook.com/help/search/?q=insights) is a free Facebook analytic tool to measure your fan growth and more.

Twitter

Twitter is a microblogging technology that is great for short pieces of information. It operates very differently from Facebook and is limited in its functions. The primary goal with Twitter is to establish *followers* of your *tweets* (written posts). As with most web technology, content is key when it comes to keeping followers engaged.

Twitter has its own powerful search technology. However, the search is limited to Twitter content, followers, and topics. Later we discuss tools to help you stay on top of your searches and tweets when maintaining your Twitter account. For now, let's get started on establishing your Twitter presence.

Ticker Shows you the things you can already see on Facebook, but in real time—instantly updating every activity of your friends or the pages you like. Keep up with the latest news as it happens.

Pinnedposts Items that admins (people who create and manage activity in groups and pages) have chosen to display prominently at the top of your brand page. A *pinned post* always appears in the top left of a page's timeline and has a flag icon in its top right corner. A post that a page admin pins to the top of the page remains there for seven days. After that, it returns to the date it was posted on the page's timeline. Posts from people who Like a page are not eligible to be pinned posts. Page admins can only pin posts they create and post within the page. Pinned posts are useful when admins wish to keep certain information or posts front and center on their pages over a period of time, while still posting new updates. This allows an admin to post relevant and timely information for prominent viewing.

1. **Set up a free Twitter account (twitter.com).** Unlike Facebook, Twitter does not separate brand from individual Twitter accounts (unless you are paying for a branded advertising page).
2. **Promote your account using your personalized Twitter profile URL.** When you create your account, as in Facebook, your username (e.g., @marthastewart) becomes part of your Twitter profile URL (so, for example, @marthastewart's Twitter profile can be found at twitter.com/marthastewart). Your Twitter profile URL links directly to your profile page and is the easiest and quickest way for others to find you. Use this link whenever possible to promote your presence on Twitter. Publicize this URL to your fans, and share it whenever you talk about Twitter. People who go to this URL and sign up for Twitter will start following you automatically.
3. **Create a Twitter button for your website** to link to your Twitter account to encourage people to follow you (twitter.com/about/resources/buttons).
4. **Make sure you appear on the search feature.** Twitter user search feature ranks search results for every user by name, username, and the bio on your profile. For your account to appear in search results, make sure your username, full name, and bio are filled out in your profile settings (twitter.com/settings) and contain keywords that

you would like to be associated with on your Twitter account. To ensure your company name appears, do a test search on your company via Twitter.

With Twitter, it is important to stay active. Tweet, retweet, and @reply/mention regularly to gain credibility among your followers so that search results are up to date and easily accessible. In Chapter 5, we discuss planning and managing Twitter content and your other social networks to stay fresh in the world of social media.

Twitter is beginning to offer different forms of advertising (support.twitter.com/articles/142101). If you are a small business, Twitter has teamed up with American Express to offer advertising (ads.twitter.com/amex).

Twitter offers *Promoted Tweets* that allow your sponsored (paid) tweets to appear in Twitter search results. Twitter also offers Promoted Trends that is an extension of Promoted Tweets, but Promoted Trends offers more search information such as time, context, and event-related items. Promoted Trends began as an extension of the Promoted Tweets platform, and is now a full-fledged product in its own right. With Promoted Trends, users see time-, context-, and event-sensitive trends promoted by advertising partners. These paid Promoted Trends appear at the top of the Trending Topics list on Twitter and are clearly marked as Promoted.

You can have a Promoted Account that helps you gain more followers by leveraging the "Who to Follow" Twitter function. Finally, Twitter has launched a Brand Page advertising opportunity, but it is currently limited to a select group of businesses (fly.twitter.com/ads).

YouTube

Now owned by Google, YouTube is the world's largest online video community. YouTube is also one of the most frequently searched websites. This makes it a prime place for marketers to reach their key audiences in a video format. Video use has exploded in recent years, and YouTube is leading the way. Not only can you access YouTube video on the web, but now you can instantly stream videos on or post videos from your mobile phone.

With YouTube, your primary goal is to get *subscribers* (Facebook has

KEY TERMS

Tweet A 140-character-maximum message that you post to the Twitter platform and that is visible to your followers and Twitter search results.

Retweet A reposting of someone else's tweet. Twitter's retweet feature helps you and others quickly share that tweet with all your followers. Sometimes people type *RT* at the beginning of a tweet to indicate they are reposting someone's content. This isn't an official Twitter command or feature, but signifies that you are quoting another user's tweet.

@Reply/Mention Any update posted by clicking the Reply button on a tweet. Your reply always begins with @*username* (insert username of the person you are replying to). Any tweet that is a reply to you begins with your username and shows up in your Mentions tab on the Connect page.

Hashtag The # symbol is used to mark keywords or topics in a tweet. It was created organically by Twitter users as a way to categorize messages. Use hashtags to categorize tweets by keyword:

- People use the hashtag symbol # before relevant keywords or phrases (no spaces) in their tweet to categorize those tweets and help them appear more easily in Twitter Search.
- Clicking on a hashtagged word in any message brings up all other tweets in that category for you to peruse.
- Hashtags can occur anywhere in the tweet.
- Hashtagged words that become popular are often *trending topics*.

fans; Twitter has followers; YouTube has subscribers), *favorites* (viewers who like your videos), and *views* (people watching your videos). The more views you get on YouTube, the higher your videos appear on viewers' searches.

Following some basic steps, you can have a commanding YouTube presence. Setting up a YouTube channel is easy. Finding enough video content for your channel, however, can be a cumbersome task.

Many companies use YouTube as a central depository for their video commercials, product videos, and instructional guides. You can set up your YouTube channel to be either private or public. Public channels are crawlable by Google (since Google owns YouTube, the platform has a robust search capability).

KEY TERM

YouTube channel Like a Facebook page or profile, or a Twitter account, a YouTube channel is the unique account or page wherein you manage your content and post videos.

1. **Set up your free YouTube channel** at youtube.com. Note: If you already have a Google account, YouTube lets you sign in with your existing ID.
2. **Create videos that address your audience's needs.** Focus your videos on information that you'd want to view if you were to land on your YouTube channel as a customer. Product videos are fine to use, as long as they address the needs of your viewers.
3. **Make your video searchable.** Your videos should be searchable both inside and outside YouTube—meaning that they will appear in search queries. To make sure your videos are able to be found in a Google or YouTube search, focus on the following key areas:
   - **Title.** Make sure your targeted keywords are in the first few words of your title.
   - **Description.** Be as complete as possible when describing your video. Imagine that you are trying to remember the name of a song you once heard. You struggle to remember the title, but you only know a couple of the verses. If you have a complete description of your video, chances are someone will find it based on the description.
   - **Tags.** These are where you enter searchable keywords. Tags are probably the most powerful search data for videos on YouTube, so be accurate.
4. **Put YouTube players on your site with your content.** It's easy to put a YouTube player from YouTube onto your own website. Just under the video, there is a sharing or Embed option. This is where you can grab (copy and paste) the HTML code to place the YouTube video on your company site—allowing that video to play directly on your website. By using YouTube videos on your site, you can acquire new subscribers, which is good for building a long-term audience.
5. **Build your own branded channel.** Create a custom background and choose your colors to match your branding. You can acquire a limited branded channel for free, including design tools, when you set up your channel. To have a full branded experience, you have to pay for it through YouTube's advertising program (youtube.com/t/advertising_brand_channels).

6. **Use annotations.** You can add *annotations* to your YouTube videos that include clickable calls to action. These annotations appear at the top of your videos for a specified time and can include links to other videos, playlists, or channels. It could also include a Subscribe option.
7. **Post a bulletin and alert your subscribers.** At the top of your channel is the Post Bulletin tab. You can create a bulletin and a link to a video that will appear on your subscribers' pages if they choose to share it. This is a great way to draw extra attention and traffic to your video.
8. **Advertise.** Yes, like the other platforms mentioned in this book, YouTube makes its money from advertising (youtube.com/yt/advertise /index.html). Advertising on YouTube through pre-video ads or text ads around the video helps your videos appear in front of more potential viewers, which ultimately helps with your ongoing strategy of gaining more subscribers.

KEY TERMS

Viewer Someone who watches a video you have posted on YouTube.

Subscriber Viewers can *subscribe* to your channel so that they can receive updates when you post new videos.

Using Google+

Recently I authored an article about Google+ for *Forbes* magazine titled "Google's Fight for the Future Web and What It Means for Brands" (forbes.com/sites/onmarketing/2012/01/05/googles-fight-for-the-future-web-and-what-it-means-for-brands).

In my opinion, at a glance, Google+ is for brands and Facebook is for friends—although read further to discover why it's not so cut and dried as the statement I just made. I believe these platforms can coexist and flourish. Facebook started as a place for friends, and when the network giant needed to create revenue, the brands came running to turn friends into

SMART MANAGING

Diversity Is the Key

One thing I have learned about social media is that there is no silver bullet when it comes to selecting a platform to market your company. You must be on several platforms to make certain you are found online. Take my advice and do both. Have a Facebook brand page and a Google+ brand page.

customers. Google, on the other hand, began as a search engine where brands list their companies, products, and services to be found by web visitors using the search engine. So opposite of Facebook, Google started with brands and is now trying to lure friends. I recommend that brands be on both platforms. No business in its right mind is going to forgo a chance to appear on Google's SERP. So if Google+ brand pages rank high on its SERP, every company will want to create a Google+ page, too.

Google+ does not allow you to customize your pages like Facebook does. Therefore, setting up your presence on Google+ is pretty simple. First, visit google.com/+/business and create your own business account. Next, begin adding your own videos, photos, and posts to make the page customized to your brand.

Circles are the most powerful feature of Google+. Instead of trying to find friends in Facebook, with Google+ your goal is to have people within your circles. With circles, you are able to group your contacts by type (friend, associates, etc.). Grouping contacts allows control over who is able to see which posts you place on Google+.

Hangouts are real-time video chats powered by Google's video engine (google.com/+/learnmore/hangouts). Using hangouts, you can conduct a video conference call with several people at once. Hangouts are new to brands, but are gaining traction quickly. Imagine a public company doing a hangout for its next earnings call. The options are plentiful, as brands can develop hangouts for sales, training, and customer service.

Hangouts can be a powerful tool if leveraged correctly. After hangouts were launched, Facebook quickly fired back by forming a partnership with Skype that allows a similar experience.

To give Google+ information on what your interests are so that it can connect you with resources, click on Sparks from the Google+ homepage. *Sparks* is where you search for things of interest and add them to your account. Get started by either browsing the categories suggested or typing your interest into the Search box. For example, I typed Ferrari in the Search box. You will see that a lot of interests have already been prepopulated into sparks, based on the results you've looked for. Click on an interest, or spark, that appeals to you. (You can choose as many as you like.) Once you have selected it, click on the Add Interest button to list it under Sparks. Add as many interests as you want, since these help connect you with other Google+ users who share your interests.

> **HANGING WITH THE PRESIDENT**
>
> FOR EXAMPLE
>
> In January 2012, President Obama hosted a hangout using Google+. Several web visitors showed up, asking him everything from helping a laid-off worker to find an engineering job (Obama asked the person to forward his résumé to him) to visitors asking him to sing and dance (which he wouldn't do).

Like Facebook's news feed, *streams* are lists of content generated by the people in your circles. Streams appear on the left side of the Google+ home page. You can either view all the streams together as one or view individual streams. To view a selected stream, click the circle name you want to filter by. When you share content on Google+, your content is added to your home page and to the home pages of people you shared with who have you in their circles.

> **SPARKS**
>
> TOOLS
>
> 1. From the Google+ home page, click on Sparks at the left under your Circles in your Stream.
> 2. Choose from the categories that Google has already set up, or type any keyword in the Search box at the top and press enter. Sparks presents you with a list of stories that the keyword brings up.
> 3. If you like the kinds of stories that appear, click Add Interest under the Search box to add it to your Sparks.
> 4. Repeat this until you have a nice list of Sparks you find interesting.
>
> **Using Sparks**
>
> 1. When you have the hankering to check out stories about a specific topic, click on that topic under your Sparks on the left on your home page.
> 2. Browse the stories and click on those you want to read. You can easily share them with your Google+ followers by clicking Share under the post excerpt (remember to use those circles to share the story with people you think might be interested).

SMART

MANAGING

Using Google+ Like a Pro

Achieving search results in Google+ is different than Facebook. On Google+, you can interact with content in one of three ways:

Like. When you click the +1 button, it is similar to saying you *like* that content. You can *plus one* on any post or comment you like to call it out and make it more visibie. Google+ Circles help you organize everyone according to your real-life social connections. Create circles for every group of people in your life from family to music buddies or alumni. Then you can share relevant content with the right people and find the content you're interested in. For example, circles let you share an engagement announcement with only your friends and family circles or find a post from a friend in your book club circle about a great new author.

Comment. When you post a *comment*, you leave your opinion or thought about that content in the thread—or chain of comments—for other users to see, including the original author. You can thank them for posting helpful information, add information, or contribute in some way.

Share. Share posts from other users directly to your own Google+ account. This is good when you have friends or users in your circles that the original poster does not have in his or her circles. By sharing content, you allow the members of your circles to participate with the content.

Finally, Google+ has a button for you to put on your site similar to Facebook's Like button. Google's *+1 button* can improve your SEO ranking on Google+ and Google's SERP. Make sure you add the +1 functionality to your own web content so users can share your content (google.com/+1/button).

KEY TERMS

Circles Groups of contacts who are accessible in your Google+ account. Circles can be organized so that you only allow access to certain people for specific information. This allows you to separate content by friends and coworkers, etc.—so that you can keep your business and personal lives separate, if desired.

Sparks Search-based interests that can be tracked and sorted into a collection of interests, allowing you to find other users with similar interests.

Streams Like Facebook's news feed, these are the areas on Google+ where your friends' information freely flows for you to read.

Earned vs. Paid Media

In the "old" days, getting listed at the top of a search engine was key. In Chapter 2, we discussed PPC (pay-per-click) and SEO (search engine optimization). As the name implies, *earned media* comes from your efforts to engage people organically on the web with compelling content. Earned media are the communication channels that broadcast your information because your site has been found organically based on its compelling content.

> **WALKING A FINE LINE BETWEEN BOMBARDMENT AND PENETRATION**
>
> SMART
>
> 
>
> MANAGING
>
> As a marketer, you want your message to penetrate your target market so that people are aware of your business. You do not, however, want to annoy your market by bombarding groups or individuals. One way to walk this fine line is to ensure that your site holds enough compelling and valuable content that potential customers find your site a resource rather than just a store.

With *paid media,* you pay to attract someone's attention. You also select the channels on which you promote your site—for example, placing banner ads or PPC text ads. They both have value but social media is usually more about "earning" attention. Table 3-1 summarizes these differences.

	Earned Media	**Paid Media**
Content	Fosters authentic conversations	Pushes information out
Connection	Drives consumer engagement	Based on a one-way, bullhorn model of broadcasting information regardless of whether the recipient asked to see it
Conversations	Organic	Focused on marketing
Scope	More targeted	Wider net
Distribution	Via multiple channels of information	Limited channels of information
Findability	Organic search engine optimization (SEO)	Paid SEO through PPC, etc.
Engagement	Enables interaction with clients and brands	Offers an introduction to goods and services

Table 3-1. Earned vs. paid media

There's a clear distinction between paid media and earned media and a time to use each. Earned media, for instance, can bring a company more credibility and foster real conversations with customers. Paid media is a good tool for companies that need to get the word out quickly via a one-way, broadcast model.

Podcasts and RSS Feeds

A *podcast* is rich media (multimedia content), such as audio or video, distributed via *RSS* to computers or mobile devices.

> **KEY TERM**
> **Rich Site Summary** (originally *RDF Site Summary*, also called *Really Simple Syndication*) is a group of web feed formats that publish frequently updated works—such as blog entries, news articles, audio, and video—in a standardized format that is readily available to subscribers.

Former MTV VJ (video jockey—like a disc jockey) Adam Curry is credited with the idea of automating the delivery and syncing of textual content with portable audio players. Listeners can retain audio archive files to listen to at their leisure. While blogs have turned many bloggers into journalists, podcasting has the potential to turn podcasters into radio personalities.

Today, through the evolution of Internet capabilities, along with cheaper hardware and software, audio podcasts are doing what was historically done through radio broadcast stations. For example, podcasting can be used for:

- **Self-guided walking tours.** Informational content
- **Music.** Band promotional clips and interviews
- **Talk shows.** Industry or organizational news, investor news, sportscasts, news coverage, commentaries
- **Training.** Instructional informational materials
- **Story.** Storytelling for children or people who are visually impaired

Now, users can either access these audios with their device from a database, or keep them in their own personal libraries—listening to or watching them while jogging, driving, or on a cross-country flight.

An RSS document (which is called a *feed*, *web feed*, or *channel*) includes full or summarized text, plus metadata such as publishing dates

Podcasting Resources

Use these resources to take advantage of podcasting in your marketing and selling initiatives:

- Podcasting tools (podcasting-tools.com)
- Podcast Alley (podcastalley.com)
- Podcasting News (podcastingnews.com)

and authorship. RSS feeds benefit publishers by letting them automatically syndicate or publish content for subscribers. A standardized XML file format allows the information to be published once and viewed on many software platforms. This benefits readers who want to subscribe to timely updates from favorite websites or to aggregate feeds from many sites in one place.

Apple the Podcaster

TRICKS OF THE TRADE

Apple is the leading resource for podcasting. To appear in the iTunes directory, register your podcast here: apple.com/itunes/podcasts/creatorfaq.html.

RSS feeds can be read using software called an RSS reader, feed reader, or aggregator, which can be web-based, desktop-based, or mobile device–based. Users subscribes to a feed by entering the feed's URL into the RSS reader or by clicking a feed icon in a web browser that initiates the subscription process. Browsers such as Safari, Chrome, etc. allow you to click on an RSS button and subscribe to content.

The RSS reader checks the user's subscribed feeds regularly for new postings, downloads any updates it finds, and provides a user interface to monitor and read the feeds. RSS lets users avoid personally inspecting all the pertinent websites and, instead, subscribe to websites with podcasts

Copyright

CAUTION

A significant issue with podcasting is copyright. It's clear that copying another's material without permission is a copyright infringement. The challenge is that podcasting technology makes copying easy. Copying a small amount may be permissible, but there is a balance to "managing" this process. The legal system gets involved when someone profits from another's work. So while all authors, writers, musicians, and others may permit some "sharing," do not abuse this.

whose new content appears on the user's browser when material becomes available.

Quick Response Codes

Developed in 1994, a *QR Code* (abbreviated from Quick Response Code) is the trademark name for a type of *matrix barcode* (a two-dimensional code) first designed for the automotive industry. The system has become widely popular due to its fast readability and large storage capacity compared to standard UPC barcodes. The code consists of black *modules* (small squares) arranged in a square pattern on a white background (Figure 3-1). You've likely seen these printed in magazine ads, posters, etc. The QR Code is also known as *mobile tagging* because smartphones can read them. When scanned, they link to digital web content, activating numerous phone functions and connecting the device to a web browser.

Figure 3. Sample QR code

MACY'S

Macy's customers were recently able use QR technology to access 30-second films showcasing Macy's celebrity designer partners. Customers could then access more content to find more information on each designer or brand. The videos are also viewable through the company's Facebook page and YouTube channel.

QR Codes have gained popularity in recent social media campaigns as they allow people to scan the code from their mobile phone and be immediately taken to a website. I've seen QR codes used in contests and on retail shelves to reveal additional product information for a potential customer.

QR codes have become a focus of advertising strategy, providing quick access to the brand's website. QR codes can be used in Google's Android operating system using Google, Goggles, or third-party barcode scanners. QR codes can be used in iOS devices via third-party barcode scanners.

Using these social media platforms and tools will enhance your ability to use online marketing effectively—allowing you to move on to the fun work of branding!

QR Code Generators

QR codes consist of black modules (square dots) arranged in a square pattern on a white background. The information encoded can be made up of four standardized kinds (modes) of data (numeric, alphanumeric, byte/binary, Kanji) or, through supported extensions, virtually any kind of data. QR Code Generators convert this data into QR codes. (Source: Denso-Wave.)

- Zxing Project (zxing.appspot.com/generator)
- BeQRious (beqrious.com/generator)
- Delivr (delivr.com/qr-code-generator)
- KAYWA (qrcode.kaywa.com)
- Likify (ikify.net)
- Shoutlet (shoutlet.com)

QR Code Readers

- Barcode Scanner (androidzoom.com/android_applications/shopping /barcode-scanner_clh.html)
- i-nigma (i-nigma.com/Downloadi-nigmaReader.html)
- Red Laser (itunes.apple.com/app/redlaser/id312720263?mt=8)
- Scan Life (web.scanlife.com/us_en)

Manager's Checklist for Chapter 3

☑ Social networks come and go quickly on the web. That's why it's important to stay maneuverable, understand today's major social tools, and watch for tomorrow's.

☑ A good social media marketing strategy leverages several social sites. This includes understanding what is unique about each platform to drive successful customer interactions.

☑ While the common thread for all social sites is similar—disseminating quality and engaging content—the tactical ways to do that vary from site to site.

☑ There are good reasons to use both earned and paid media to gain attention, but the process is different for each. Both require quality and engaging content, but earned media requires thoughtful action, while paid media requires thoughtful placement.

☑ Podcasting is an effective way to share content in social circles.

 QR codes make sharing content easier, and keywords improve customers' ability to find content online and can be effectively tied into your social media campaigns.

Personal Branding

Personal branding is about managing your name—even if you don't own a business—in a world of misinformation, disinformation, and semi-permanent Google records. Going on a date? Chances are that your "blind" date has Googled your name. Going to a job interview? Ditto. —Tim Ferriss, Author, *The 4-Hour Work Week*

Now more than ever, when it comes to your personal "brand," it's important to manage your *digital trail,* or the information online about you and your online reputation. While most people don't want to be found online for privacy reasons, it's becoming increasingly easy to find information about anyone—even you—online.

For brand marketers, however, being found online is less of a nuisance or concern. In fact, it is an imperative for many who want to become known as experts. For that reason, establishing a social presence online is critical in becoming an online thought leader.

Whether you are trying to build a company, get a new job, or sell a product, the person with the highest number of fans, followers, subscribers, or people in his or her circle wins. This chapter focuses on helping you set up your digital presence from ground zero.

I'm not going to sugarcoat it for you: Becoming an online expert is tough business. You have to always be "on" and always creating new content in the form of a post, tweet, video, etc. For many, it's a full-time job and it quickly becomes tiresome. Starting and stopping an online thought leadership presence is worse than not starting up at all.

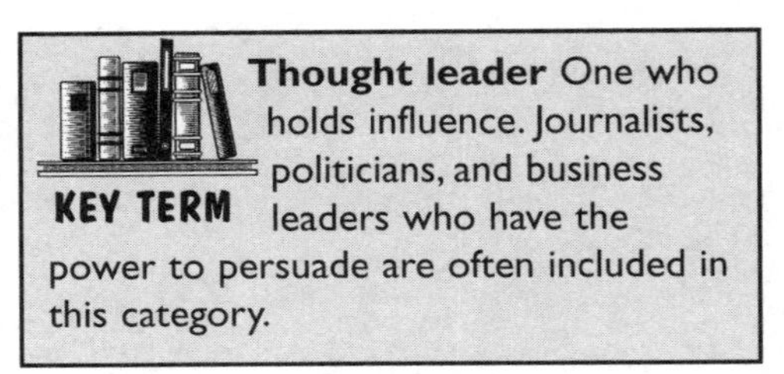

KEY TERM

Thought leader One who holds influence. Journalists, politicians, and business leaders who have the power to persuade are often included in this category.

We explore strategies and tactics to help you with the initial phases of personal branding, as well as examine social platforms and tools to help you maintain your presence once you start.

Establishing Yourself as an Expert

Let's define *expert* before we go too far. An *expert* is someone who knows his or her content exceptionally well.

SMART MANAGING

EXPERT VS. THOUGHT LEADER

You can be an expert without being a thought leader. Being an expert requires mere knowledge, while being a thought leader requires being found and respected by others for that knowledge. Strive to be a thought leader online.

This chapter will help you establish an online presence by leveraging online tools so you attract more people to your brand. You can choose to be an expert in any industry. I've helped many clients establish their online expertise in several industries from industrial waste, to electronics manufacturing, to baked goods. Whatever industry you are in now, chances are someone is already considered a thought leader in your space and can be found online today.

KEY TERM

Personal branding The process whereby people and their careers are marked as a brand.

We touched on branding in an earlier chapter. Now we are going to back up and talk about personal branding as it pertains to building your business and online presence.

The personal branding concept suggests that even business success comes first from self-packaging—that is, positioning yourself as a thought leader. In August 1997, Tom Peters, coauthor of *In Search of Excellence*, published an article in *Fast Times* magazine titled "The Brand

TRICKS OF THE TRADE

WHAT DO "YOU" HAVE TO DO WITH IT?

Why would you worry about personal branding if your goal is to market a business? Because by building your personal brand, you broaden your platform and reach. As a thought leader who represents a company or idea, you can market your products or ideas to those who already respect you for the content, relationships, or experiences you bring. You also build a brand (yourself) that may outlast the company you work for or the product or service you sell.

Called You" (fastcompany.com/magazine/10/brandyou.html). In the article, Peters suggested you treat yourself as a product and position yourself just as you would sell an item to the world.

The concept of personal branding has increased exponentially through social media. Sites like Facebook and its news feed have become popular because people love to talk about themselves.

DON'T CONFUSE PERSONAL BRANDING WITH BRAGGING

CAUTION

While personal branding involves some of the same tools you might use in business marketing—such as Facebook—it is not done for merely personal purposes. Bragging about your two-year-old who already knows how to write books might gain you some semijealous props (recognition) from Facebook friends but does little to brand you as an expert on the topic of your business (unless your business happens to be training toddlers to read and write). Personal branding powers your professional brand, not your personal preferences. It involves leveraging some personal information and creating many personal relationships—but doing so in a way that is consistent with the goals, values, and objectives of your business brand.

Over the past few years, I've seen a variety of ways to leverage social media for your personal brand. Some tactics are more complex than others. Specifically, starting a blog is more difficult to maintain because of the continuous demand for long-form content. Therefore, platforms like Twitter have emerged that are easier to maintain since your communication is limited to 140 characters.

In Chapter 3, we reviewed how to set up social sites such as Facebook, Twitter, and YouTube. In this chapter, we focus on social platforms geared to individual branding.

LinkedIn

LinkedIn is the world's largest social network for online professionals. The site's primary focus is to help business professionals network through their existing connections. LinkedIn can be an incredible resource for establishing your online presence and meeting new connections. If you don't already have a LinkedIn account, you can get one easily (linkedin.com). I recommend filling out your profile as completely as possible. Based on the information you enter, LinkedIn recommends connections connected to where you went to school, where you work, and where you live.

LinkedIn as a destination. Consider using your profile as a *destination*—meaning a place you refer people to in order to learn more about you. If you have a corporate website, add a link to your personal LinkedIn profile so visitors to your website can connect with you quickly. Also consider adding the URL to your LinkedIn profile on your business cards and e-mail signature (get the LinkedIn button here: linkedin.com/profile/profile badges). You'll find people are quick to send you a LinkedIn invitation to make you one of their connections.

Linking external content to your LinkedIn profile. By using the available tools (like LinkedIn, Twitter, etc.) to link to your blog or Twitter feed, or to create polls, you can share helpful information with this network to be passed along through others' networks to create new connection opportunities for you or your business. Many *third-party applications* (such as Foursquare, a location-sharing service/tool that helps you keep up with friends, discover new places, and get deals and discounts) allow you to post to LinkedIn when you interact with their applications. This continuous posting will appear in the LinkedIn Updates area, similar to Facebook's news feed or Google+ streams. Linking external content to your LinkedIn profile drives traffic to your page and encourages people to connect with you.

KEY TERM
Third-party application
A tool used to complement a social media vehicle, website, or device to achieve a specific purpose.

Leverage your expertise on LinkedIn Groups and Answers. LinkedIn *Groups* and *Answers* are a great way to identify other users with similar interests

LinkedIn groups Groups on LinkedIn, usually relating to a subject or company, where message board discussions are held, jobs are posted, and people connect. It is helpful to join groups in your subject area, or with companies or organizations with which you wish to network. You can search for LinkedIn groups to identify those you want.

LinkedIn Answers LinkedIn Answers lets you tap the knowledge of your professional network. You ask a question via LinkedIn and then you receive answers from your connections, their connections, and experts who use LinkedIn. People answer your question. In addition, you can find questions to answer in your areas of expertise. You can either provide your own answers or recommend connections who can help. Experts are featured on the Answers home page, and in each category of questions.

and needs. By providing useful information to others you improve your own reputation as an expert resource on select topics. One of the best ways to establish yourself as an expert on a particular topic is to participate in others' posts.

Consider establishing a group on LinkedIn. Last year my company began a LinkedIn group, Social Commerce: Selling with Social Media. Now the group has thousands of participants contributing hundreds of articles and posts each month. The group is almost maintenance free since the members are the content contributors. My company is able to maintain our position as the industry expert on this topic simply because we manage the group (and are now seen as a thought leader).

Twitter

Even though we covered Twitter in the previous chapter, we revisit it here to discuss personal branding. Most people in my company have a personal Twitter account, as do I, aside from a corporate Twitter account. Even though a business account is set up the same way as a personal account, the tone of these two accounts should be different.

For corporate Twitter accounts, keep your tweets informational. You comment and retweet more often about your industry events than you would in a personal account. A corporate account can also link to *e-commerce sites* if you're selling a product or service. Twitter has a downloadable guide for small businesses (business.twitter.com/en/basics/best-practices) that contains valuable information on best practices for companies looking to use Twitter.

MAKE TWEETS APPROPRIATE

Be careful not to create too casual a tone if your intention is to become a thought leader through your personal tweets.

TWEETING BLOGS

If you're writing a blog, consider putting the Twitter button on your posts to allow easy linking of your content onto Twitter (twitter.com/about/resources/buttons).

Personal accounts should be a reflection of yourself.

Several industry experts have both personal and business Twitter accounts set up, but they know how to leverage each for different purposes.

About.me

Several *personal page platforms*—or systems for organizing social media profiles and information—have emerged to help you consolidate your social media connections. About.me (https://about.me) is one of the largest platforms available that lists links. AOL purchased About.me only four days after its public launch.

About.me lets you create a personal branded page with a few clicks. These personalized pages contain links to your Twitter account, LinkedIn profile, etc. Think of this as your personal landing page. You can view my About.me personal page here: about.me/mixdown.

Since companies like About.me want to drive more traffic to their platform, they make it easy for search engines to find you. Getting found gets you noticed, and getting noticed gets you one step closer to becoming an industry expert.

There are other sites like About.me that you could also join. Both Flavors.me (flavors.me) and Xeeme (xeeme.com) share similar features. It's too early to tell which platform will win the personal page race, so I suggest joining them all. Don't worry, these platforms are a "set it and forget it" type of service that doesn't require much, if any, updating once they are established.

Measuring Your Influence

Several platforms offer ways to measure online influence. Each platform has a different formula for how influence is measured, so it's important to evaluate each and determine which platform best aligns with your beliefs in how online influence should be measured.

Klout

The *Klout Score* (klout.com) measures your influence based on your ability to drive or influence the actions of other users. Every time you create content or engage with others, you influence others. The Klout Score uses data from social networks to measure the following:

- **True Reach.** Your *True Reach* is the number of people you reach. It filters out spam and bots (automated robots) and focuses on the people who are acting on your content.
- **Amplification.** Your *Amplification* is how much you influence people. When you post a message, how many people respond to it or share it? If people often act on your content, then you have a high Amplification score.
- **Network.** Your *Network* indicates the influence of the people in your True Reach. How often do top *influencers* share and respond to your content? When they do so, they increase your Network score.

Many online influencers continually work to earn more Klout. Klout awards points as you increase your social connections by adding your Facebook, Twitter, Foursquare, and LinkedIn accounts to your Klout score. Obviously, Klout is trying to become the standard in online influence measurement. However, Klout has some competition. Platforms like PeerIndex and TwitterGrader want you to be tied into their tracking service. If your goal is to become visible online, I recommend joining each of them. It's a lot of work in the beginning, but you never know which platform will give you the most visibility.

Measuring Online Influence

Listed here are the current tools available for measuring online influence. I recommend giving each of them a try.

- PeerIndex (peerindex.net)
- Tweetlevel (tweetlevel.edelman.com)
- Twitalyzer (twitalyzer.com)
- How Sociable (howsociable.com)
- Postrank (postrank.com)
- TwitterGrader (twittergrader.com)

Blogs and Microblogging

Blogs are one of the earliest forms of social media and the most widely used. Twitter is a *microblogging* (abbreviated form of blogging) tool that has achieved its own brand, just as Kleenex took over tissues. Blogging has given a voice to millions of writers and will continue to have a major impact on new media (rich media) and the magazine publishing industry—in that now much of the content that used to only appear in print can appear online in blogs. Today, some of the most widely read bloggers are magazine reporters and writers, which shows us that it's about content quality and engaging material.

WANT TO BE AN AUTHOR? BECOME A BLOGGER

You've probably heard stories of bloggers who developed hundreds of thousands of fans, and then were contacted by publishing companies for book deals. While this isn't an everyday occurrence, it does happen. If you can attract a large readership online as a thought leader to your blog, you may be able to attract buyers to a book! Even if you don't land a publishing deal, writing a blog can help you refine your thoughts so that you can promote your service or expertise or tell your story.

Blogging software has matured to become more than just a "blog," but also a *content management system* that can be used to manage an entire website. These solutions typically are easier to use and low cost, if not free (with advertising supporting it).

Content management system (CMS) A platform through which you can manage the content of your website.

Here is a look at the two largest providers:

Blogger

One of the first blogging software developers started in San Francisco under the name of Pyra Labs in 1999. Like a lot of start-ups they had a rocky beginning, but by 2002 they had hundreds of thousand users, enough to attract Google's attention.

With the backing of and access to the tremendous resources of Google, Blogger has become a dominant player while keeping costs low.

Blogger's key features are ease of use, flexible hosting, and security and reliability of the platform.

WordPress

WordPress is a platforrm for bloggers that started in 2003 with a single bit of code to enhance the typography of everyday writing and with fewer users than you can count on your fingers and toes. WordPress made it easy for bloggers to write, edit, and publish their entries for anyone online to view.

> **BLOGGING COMMUNITIES** SMART MANAGING
>
> Like social media, blogging communities offer a chance to share your ideas and posts with others and meet like-minded people. Not only that, they're all dedicated to one thing, blogging.

Since then, WordPress has grown into the largest self-hosted blogging tool in the world, used on millions of sites and seen by tens of millions of people every day. WordPress was created by and for the blogging community. WordPress is an *open source project,* which means there are hundreds of people all over the world working on improving it.

Because of the large open community, users have access to hundreds of free *plugins* and *themes* (see definitions on following page), and for reasonable fees, users also have access to hundreds of professional themes. WordPress is also particularly strong with SEO.

> **WORDPRESS—BEYOND BLOGGING** TRICKS OF THE TRADE
>
> Today many companies use the WordPress platform to manage the content of their websites—because it is inexpensive and easy to learn—negating much of the expense of building an online presence. Additionally, without having much web experience, users can log in to change web copy instantly. Many web designers, formerly hired to run websites, are now being asked to help set up these do-it-yourself options—providing support while users do much of the work themselves.

Blogging Best Practices

Follow these best practices when startingand writing a blog:

- **Blog consistently.** Starting and then discontinuing your blog is worse than not starting one at all.

KEY TERMS

Themes Design templates for websites. Users who install a theme can customize it with their content, graphics, and more. Thousands of themes exist—many of them customized by industry or purpose to make your web publishing job easier and less expensive (often bypassing the need for a highly skilled graphic designer or web programmer for the site's design).

Plugins Add-ons to WordPress that increase functionality in a particular area. For example, there are plugins to enhance the use of YouTube videos on a website or to allow for easy gathering of e-mail addresses to incorporate into a newsletter list. Plugins can be downloaded and installed.

- **Add social sharing components** to your blog so articles and posts can be passed along within readers' social networks—opening the door for a viral response.
- **Check** for typos and check all your facts. If you don't, you'll get called out quickly.
- **Guest post** on other blogs, if permission is granted.
- **Make your content interesting** so people will return to your blog to see what's coming next.

SMART

MANAGING

Guest Blogging

Becoming a guest blogger is a good way to get your content out to like-minded readers and expand your number of followers. Your personal branding becomes powerful in guest blogging efforts. If you have a strong network, ask other bloggers if they would consider running a guest post from you. If they agree, write on a topic that interests the host blogger—and be respectful of meeting their deadlines and guidelines. Offer to reciprocate—giving the host blogger exposure on your blog as well. Ask to have a link to your blog posted in your guest entry, so that readers can find your site as well—and offer this in return to those whose content you accept.

Getting Ready to Blog

Domain Name

1. Find out what domain names (URLs) are available to name your blog. Go to Network Solutions.com, GoDaddy.com, or Dotster.com.
2. Register your domain name. You can keep the name for up to 10 years.
3. Consider domain forwarding—that is, having a domain redirect to

another domain after it is entered (something you set up through your host); and domain masking. Masking, sometimes called domain mapping, can be helpful if your name of choice is not available, in that once the site is up, it shows a different URL often more targeted to the name you wish to brand.

Hosting

The second part of starting a blog is hosting. Blog hosting is different from website hosting as it includes blogging software but not other features of web hosting such as e-mail. Some providers like WordPress are offer both web and blog hosting.

Building Fans and Followers

People often ask me about strategies to build their company and individual fan bases. There is no silver bullet when it comes to social media. Gaining true fans is a result of several tactics, great content, and old-fashioned hard work.

> **DOMAIN MAPPING** — TRICKS OF THE TRADE
>
> Domain mapping is a feature you can use to point multiple domains to your primary hosting account. You can map domain names to any desired location within your hosting. For example you can map a domain to a blog folder so that the domain goes the blog page. When a domain is mapped to a hosting package, the hosted website will be visible by going to that domain name.

Advertise for Friends

Use advertising to acquire new fans (via display banners, keyword ads, Facebook ads, etc.) and to drive traffic to your social media channels. Be sure you ask people to either "fan" or "like" your Facebook page, follow you on Twitter, or subscribe to your YouTube channel, depending on your goal. Having a *call to action* (a request for the user to do something in response to seeing your material) in your advertising and on your website is key to getting your money's worth when paying for advertising.

> **FOSTERING EVANGELISTS** — SMART MANAGING
>
> Fans are great, and imperative for growth in social media. Even better are evangelists—those who take your message to a new level by recruiting more fans to your page. Foster evangelists, and your page will grow while you sleep.

Ask Your Coworkers, Friends, and Family to Follow You

Send a targeted e-mail to everyone you know asking them to "friend" your page, follow you on Twitter, etc. Most of your friends have other friends who would want to connect with you. Don't forget to add Facebook or Twitter addresses to the bottom of your company's e-mail signature.

Provide an Incentive to Follow You

A friend recently celebrated his small advertising agency's birthday. To gain new fans, he posted on the news feed, "It's our birthday. Fan our page today and I'll give you free movie tickets." Clearly, he had to cap the offer after a certain time or number of tickets, but needless to say, it was a clever strategy for gaining more fans quickly.

Sponsors

If you are really savvy and motivated, take the free ticket option a step farther. If you have enough fans to make it worthwhile to a "sponsor," you can contact a business and ask them to donate a small prize (such as those free movie tickets) in exchange for promoting them on your page. Ask the business specifically what sort of mention they would like and agree to a frequency for your mention of them—and a format (status updates giving them a shout-out, a posted graphic or video, etc.). Then, offer this sponsor's prize to users for responding on Facebook to a contest or other query. This can only be done on business pages, and not on personal profiles, due to Facebook's promotion regulations.

Answer Others' Questions

Browse Twitter, Facebook, YouTube, and other sites. Comment on others' posts and content. Show you are a thought leader by helping others. I recall a time I landed one of my biggest clients simply because I commented on a book on Amazon. The company executive liked my opinion, found me through LinkedIn, and hired me for a consulting project. Make certain you are active on others' blogs, Twitter posts, etc. You'll be amazed how quickly you pick up your own new followers.

Make Friends with Influencers

Influential people are on the social networks. If you are a professional and respected by these influential people online, typically they will help you gain recognition. I was surprised at how accessible famous people are online. I remember when Walt Mossberg, editor of the *Wall Street Journal* Technology Section, responded to me on Twitter. Reach out and make friends. They can help you get in front of millions.

> **DON'T BUY FANS**
>
> CAUTION
>
> Do not use services to purchase fans or followers for your Facebook or Twitter accounts. Many of these services spam web visitors or use your account to friend people you do not know. There is no true way to buy friends, so don't try it.

Keep a Flow of Consistent Content

If you run out of things to say, people will forget about you. Having an ongoing flow of useful content and information allows you to stay connected to your fans and followers. In Chapter 5, we discuss creating an editorial calendar to help you maintain your online presence.

Automating Content

There's no way to automate content creation—meaning to have a robot or program write compelling copy for you—but there are some strategies that will make your job easier. First, I do not recommend that you automate every post, every blog entry, and every Tweet. On the social web, authenticity reigns, so it's important to make sure you don't automate too much or you will come across as being "spammy" and quickly lose your audience. Even worse, you risk the possibility of getting banned from certain websites and social networks. So please, use the following strategies with caution. In the end, the more personalized you make an interaction, the deeper your relationship will become with your fans and followers.

Yahoo! Pipes

In my opinion, Yahoo! Pipes (pipes.yahoo.com/pipes) is an underused technology and should be more popular than it is. In essence, Yahoo! Pipes is a content aggregation tool. It allows you to pull in content from practically any website and manipulate (edit and change) it to be distributed on other sites or social networks—such as your own. As a user, you create *pipes* that can funnel content anywhere. There is a good tutorial video on the Yahoo! Pipes site that shows you how to set up the free service for yourself. Try using a pipe to automate keywords to appear in your Twitter posts, to help in your branding and SEO. View a list of popular pipes here: pipes.yahoo.com/pipes/pipes.popular. You can create various combinations to automate content aggregation to make your social website content appear fresh by continuously pulling in content from outside sources.

RSS Feeds

RSS is a way to syndicate content automatically or summarize content into a format available to people by subscription.

RSS benefits readers who want to subscribe to timely updates from favorite websites or to aggregate feeds from many sites into one place. RSS feeds can be read using software called an *RSS reader*. Google has a great web-based RSS reader that lets you combine your inbound RSS feed subscriptions into a compilation of information for reading later (google.com/reader).

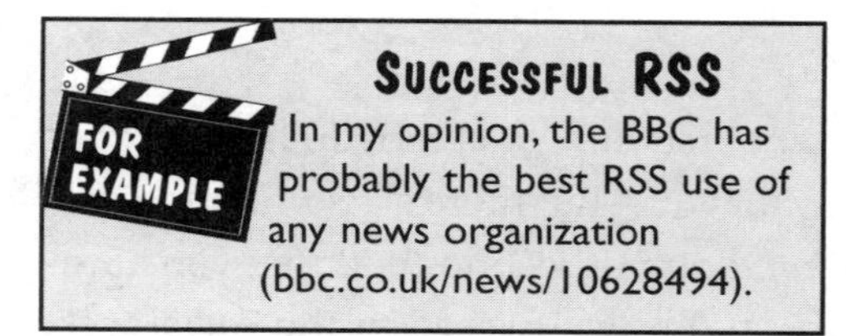

SUCCESSFUL RSS

In my opinion, the BBC has probably the best RSS use of any news organization (bbc.co.uk/news/10628494).

Publishing RSS is easy when using tools designed to create feeds. Feedburner and Shoutlet offer robust ways to create and track RSS feeds that you publish so that you can measure your feed analytics.

Like Yahoo! pipes, you can set up RSS to automatically collect content and place it into your website or blog. This process is often referred to as *broadcatching*. You can grab RSS content from most major news sites today.

CONTENT CREATION

Content creation has been a challenge for many organizations. Platforms like CrowdContent (crowdcontent.com) and Animoto (animoto.com) have emerged on the scene that promise to help you with content creation. Animoto automatically creates videos for you just by uploading a handful of images. The platform is winning several industry awards. It's neat to see it work—I recommend giving it a try.

Branding yourself as a thought leader becomes a valuable way to brand your business. When well thought out, blogging is a valuable tool to help in your overall branding.

Manager's Checklist for Chapter 4

- ☑ Be careful what you post online. Remember: you are what you Tweet.
- ☑ The key to becoming an industry expert is having compelling content and a commanding presence online via platforms like LinkedIn.
- ☑ Post on others' blogs, comments, and networks to gain followers.
- ☑ Starting a blog is a full-time job. Make sure you have a plan before you begin.
- ☑ Approach content automation with caution.

Planning

The aim of marketing is to know and understand the customer so well the product or services fits him and sells itself.

—Peter Drucker, author, professor, and management consultant

Many marketing people looking to take their strategies online for the first time have what I call Inflated Expectation Syndrome when it comes to online marketing. This means many marketing people think online is free and you'll sell millions of dollars of your products or services just by putting up a company Facebook page. Beginning online marketers think their campaign is going to take off like wildfire with no effort or advertising. They think their content is the next "dancing baby," "lonely girl 15," or "evolution of dance" video that will rip through the Internet and drive thousands to their e-commerce site to buy their products. Sadly, online success isn't that easy. Like everything in life, online marketing takes careful planning, hard work, and perfect timing.

In this chapter, we take a detailed approach to planning your online marketing strategy. We examine the resources required to execute a true online marketing strategy, whether you are a part-time employee doing online marketing on the side or the vice president of digital marketing exploring new ideas for your next campaign.

START WHERE YOU ARE

Don't set goals that are so ambitious that you can't achieve them. Measure your progress as you proceed with your online marketing. Be realistic with your timelines for accomplishing new social media outreach and metrics. Setting yourself up for success rather than failure will keep you motivated to continue.

Researching Your Online Audience

I always tell my clients to "begin with the end in mind." Visualize what you feel would constitute success from your online marketing campaign before you start. It sounds simple, but it's actually a big step for most marketers. I've been onsite with clients on several occasions where we explored their objectives and never arrived at a solid decision on what they would deem a successful campaign. In fact, it happened so often that I created a worksheet for new clients titled "What Success Will Look Like."

A short time ago, I worked with leaders of a large medical equipment company helping them enter social media. They wanted to target anesthesiologists (in this chapter, I prove to you that everyone is online!) who were looking to upgrade the machines at their hospitals. In our initial meeting, we went over their current marketing efforts and looked at ways to leverage their offline strategies to gain momentum online.

In the meeting, I pressed them for a definition of success. I would not let up on the topic until I received a straight answer. In my experience, success needs to be defined and mutually agreed on before a business relationship begins. I have found that it's too easy to rush through an introductory period and find out later that expectations were not met because of miscommunication. Since so many marketers have Inflated Expectation Syndrome, I needed to get a definition to keep them grounded. The group kept generalizing success as "increased number of Facebook fans," "increased awareness online," "more traffic to our website," etc.

Finally I asked, "After this campaign is over, how will you know you've won?" One woman was bold enough to say, "We would have sold more machines to anesthesiologists." Bingo! Working backward, we discovered they needed to sell more machines. The best way to sell machines was to set up events in several cities and invite local anesthesiologists. From those events, they could track every lead until a sale occurred. My sugges-

> **IT'S ALL ABOUT SALES**
>
> 
>
>
> Chances are, if you are reading this book, someone or several people in your organization are concerned about bringing in revenue—whether in the form of sales, donations, or grants. Perhaps (and hopefully) one of those people is you. While social media may be deemed a "fun" experiment for many, it also has a concrete purpose within online marketing: to generate revenue. This revenue may come indirectly through building your corporate brand or reputation, making customers happier and more loyal (think repeat business), or positioning your site so that potential customers find you before your competitors. The increased revenue could come directly from the sales you generate from your Facebook links, etc. Either way, if you are running a business (rather than a hobby), keep the goal in mind: making sure that social media supports overall revenue-building efforts.

tion was to focus on getting more attendees to each event. Since I couldn't physically sell each piece of equipment for them, my responsibility stopped once a qualified anesthesiologist showed up at a local event. The rest was on them. We had defined success.

The process of finding and targeting your online audience is a challenge, but not impossible by any means. In the years that I've been working in the online marketing space, I've never, not once, failed to find a client's target audience online. There are several strategies you can use to find out who your audience is, where they are online, and what type of content they would like to receive. We explore all these methods in this chapter.

Finding Influencers

Whomever you are trying to reach, you can find them online. Whether you want to reach baking enthusiasts (bakespace.com), irritable bowel syndrome sufferers (ibstales.com), or you are a "furry" and like to dress up in an animal costume (furry4life.org), there is a place online for you. Best of all, as a marketer, the social web makes it even easier to find your target audience online. Social networks make it easier for marketers to target potential buyers in that users list all their interests, likes/dislikes, marital status, age, race, location, etc. Sites like Facebook have become an open book for individuals to express themselves and find others with similar interests online in seconds. The key is understanding how to

Do Unto Others

When culling sites for information, be conscious in your correspondence with potential new clients of how they may perceive your efforts. It doesn't pay to spam or send over-the-top solicitations. Keep your correspondence conversational and respectful.

quickly filter through all your options to find the holy grail—your ideal customer—through these websites and social networks.

Locating Your Audience

It's not that tough to locate your audience. People tend to overthink the process of finding their online audience. Here are some options for finding your audience:

Use a simple Google search to find your audience online. You read that correctly. Just Google various combinations of your audience's job title and keywords. For example: "picnics," "eating outside," "grilling," "BBQs," "finger foods," "outside snacks," etc., if you are trying to reach those interested in picnicking. Or type in "anesthesiology equipment" in the example I introduced in this chapter. Think of all the possible combinations your audience might use to search for your products. Then sort those returns into communities and blogs where they might be online. This works especially well for consumer product companies.

TRICKS OF THE TRADE

Shopping the Competition

Research whom your competitors and others in the industry are talking to, and reach out to those companies or people. Go to the "clients" pages of businesses that serve your industry to gain ideas for those who might also become buyers of your product or service.

Use social media monitoring tools to find out where online conversations are taking place. Today, both free and paid social media monitoring tools exist. Tools like Social Mention (socialmention.com) are free, while a tool like Radian6 (radian6.com) is a paid tool and slightly more powerful for monitoring conversations. Using social media monitoring tools will give you a deeper look into real-time conversations based on a keyword search. In a short time, you begin to find where genuine conversations are taking place. That will give you a better understanding of which sites you want to advertise on or which sites you want to partner with in your

Qualifying Partners

When qualifying blog sites to determine if they would be beneficial to partner with, consider these qualities and features of influential blogs:

- The content of the blog matches your product or brand's niche.
- Social media monitoring has uncovered that the blog or its readers are discussing your brand or a topic related to your brand.
- The blog contains frequent posts (minimum of a couple times a week).
- The blog experiences high unique monthly traffic. (Run the numbers at Compete.com.) Visitors stay on the site (the longer the better). (Again, run the numbers at Compete.com.)
- The average number of comments per post is high.
- The blog roll is substantial and targeted to your topic. (A blog roll is a list of other blogs that the blog author reads or recommends—usually appearing beside the blog.)
- The number of link-backs to the site is high. (Run the numbers at Technorati.com or Alexa.com.)
- The outbound links included in the blog posts are frequent, influential, and targeted.
- Is the blog doing nonsponsored product reviews? The blogger should not be paid to post.
- The advertisers on the blog are appropriate for its content and readership.

social media efforts. To qualify a partner, make sure your target audience is being directed to the page. Then contact the company to get advertising rates or discuss partnership opportunities.

Finding a specific audience like anesthesiologists is more difficult, but possible. It seems that in almost every speech I give, someone in the audience challenges me about working in social media for companies that sell to other businesses (B2B, or business-to-business). Anytime I've been backed into a corner about finding an audience as tough as anesthesiologists, I ask them, "Which associations does your company belong to?" I've never encountered a company that sold products or services to other businesses that didn't have a few associations to which they belonged. With the medical company I mentioned earlier, they were quick to rattle off three associations that they were involved with. I recommended to the company that they ask those associations if they could survey association members regarding social media use. More often than not, these associations are so curious about what their members' responses would be to the questions below that they allow the company to do the survey for free in exchange for a copy of the results. You'd be amazed what information you can uncover about your audience if you ask them. In the survey, we asked the target audience three simple questions:

1. Where do you hang out online?
2. What kind of content do you like to receive?
3. How can we most effectively reach you?

Try paid searches. You have the option of paid advertising to locate your audience. Google and Facebook make it easy to find people online using paid keyword advertising (pay-per-click or PPC). Often they can estimate your reach before you spend any money with them. This is one of the best ways to get in front of your audience, as keyword advertising has turned into a multibillion-dollar industry.

IDENTIFYING INFLUENCERS

The following is a list of tools to help you identify where your influencers are online.

- Follower Wonk (followerwonk.com)
- Tweet Grader (tweet.grader.com)
- Twellow (twellow.com)
- Klout (klout.com)
- Technorati (technorati.com)
- Google+ Statistics (socialstatistics.com)

FOR EXAMPLE

CASE STUDY: REACHING TRUCKERS

A manufacturer of semitrucks was looking for its target audience online: owner/operators who can purchase an expensive semi. We used social media monitoring tools to determine where those truckers were online. We found more than 1.2 million semi drivers on various blogs, groups, and trucker-focused websites. We surveyed these truckers and asked them, "What kind of content do you want to receive?" "How would you like to receive it?" We discovered that the truckers wanted to receive information about nutrition and exercise. We were able to create branded content that was well received.

The surprising information was how they wanted to receive the content. We learned that more than 90 percent of the truckers surveyed had iPods or iPhones. The distribution method became immediately clear; we developed a series of podcasts that were accessible anytime for this on-the-go audience.

Resource and Staff Planning

If you are like most of my clients, you're probably just beginning to build a social media team. Over the past few years, I've seen departments range from a part-time intern managing a digital strategy to a team of eight full-time social media professionals. Every organization operates differently and each company has access to different resources. Whatever your situation, it is possible to create a plan that fits your organization.

No Resources/Small Team

The part-time option is where many companies begin, so let's start there. If you're a company of one or don't have the budget to hire a digital marketing team, there are still ways to leverage online marketing effectively. You can develop low-maintenance strategies. Creating strategies that require a lot of your time or tons of content will quickly overwhelm you. Remember that it's worse to start and stop than never to begin an online presence. Listed are some items to consider when starting small:

Create a self-running group on LinkedIn or Facebook. One of the smartest things we did at our company before we had access to a team was to create a LinkedIn group and open it to other people. In doing so, we maintained our company brand in front of thousands of marketing professionals while they posted all the content. It was easy to get attention when we wanted to promote an upcoming white paper or webinar. Since we controlled the group, we could post whatever we wanted to the page.

Understand the time commitment of starting a blog. I often joke to my speaking audiences about my wife's desire to start a journal where she records the daily interactions of our three children. She begins the journal every year in January and then abandons it by March. Maintaining a blog is too much work to do it part-time. Blogs are normally long-form text and they need to be fed continuously. You'll overwhelm yourself with all the information required to make it *sticky*—attractive enough to engage your customers.

Send tweets. Twitter is low maintenance. You are limited to 140 characters, so you can't write a novel on it. Additionally, there is retweeting, which I personally love. Twitter lets you share articles from websites like the *New York Times* within seconds. Lastly, you can automate some of your tweets using Yahoo! Pipes, as described in Chapter 4.

Some Resources/Medium Team

You're establishing a digital marketing team and have access to resources to kick-start your effort. Often I meet with companies that have a public relations person, an advertising person, an e-commerce person, a brand manager, or a marketing director. More often than not, they are already overwhelmed with their existing workload and now their boss has dumped "figuring out digital marketing and social media" on their laps. Sound like you? Well, there is hope. My suggestion for groups in this position is to form a digital media/social media committee. Agree to dedicate 5 percent of your time to digital media, dividing up responsibilities based on individual expertise. Agree to meet at least weekly (preferably on Fridays so you don't get distracted with routine tasks and can develop a plan for the following week before heading home for the weekend). Try to never miss a meeting or reschedule. Here are some tips for your new committee to get started in digital marketing and social media:

- **Create success metrics.** Remember to define "what success will look like" before you begin. It's better for everyone if you have a clear understanding of what success in digital marketing means before you begin. Start with your goal in mind and work backward.
- **Develop a routine.** At the committee's initial meeting, determine your objectives. Consider exactly what each staff member will contribute to the group every week. Evaluate tasks by individual expertise and interest, and align a plan that works with staff schedules. Create and distribute an agenda before each meeting and never end a meeting without defined action steps for the next week.
- **Repurpose content.** Several companies have quality content available in public relations or marketing pieces that can be used in social media. I've seen companies take sections of their published newsletters and reformat them into an RSS feed reader, then distribute it on their blog, Facebook page, and website in a shareable web applica-

tion. Look for videos, stories, or audio clips to repurpose into your social media channels.

Shareable Web Applications

The following Shoutlet apps (see Shoutlet.com for more) will help you distribute your content in a manner that others can share:

Photo Contests Module. Add a comprehensive photo contest to a Facebook tab (Figure 5-1). All of Shoutlet's contest options include a full set of contest management features, voting, social sharing, and tracking.

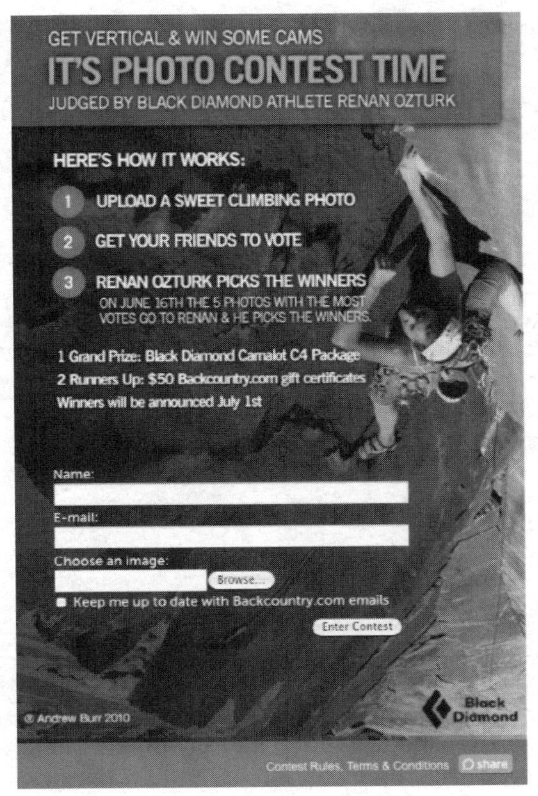

Figure 5-1. Photo contest module

RSS Reader Web App. Pull any RSS feed into an RSS reader web app that is socially shareable and easily customizable (Figure 5-2).

Figure 5-2. RSS reader web app

Twitter Web App. Syndicate a Twitter feed, Twitter search results, or a #hashtag stream to a shareable web app (Figure 5-3).

Figure 5-3. Twitter web app

Sign-Up Web App. Allow users to input personal information on your tab, such as name, e-mail, street address, phone, and Twitter username—perfect for gathering newsletter registrations (Figure 5-4).

Figure 5-4. Sign-up web app

Use Your Own Web App. Upload a Flash file or image to display your content in a shareable web app (Figure 5-5).

Figure 5-5. Use your own web app

Coupon Module. Include any Shoutlet-hosted coupon image and make it clickable as well (Figure 5-6).

Figure 5-6. Coupon module

Video Podcast Player. Create video podcast feeds and easily add new video files for new episodes to a shareable, customizable web app (Figure 5-7).

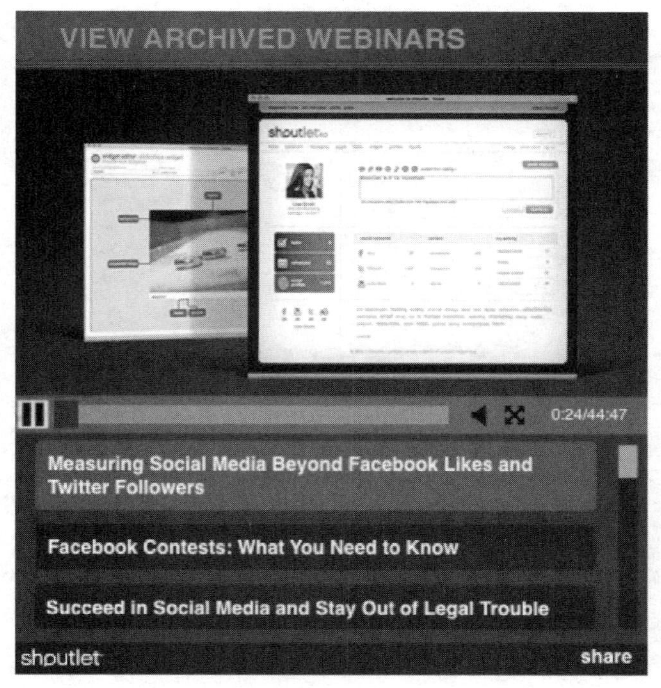

Figure 5-7. Video podcast player

Video Player. Add video via a branded, shareable Shoutlet-powered video player that clicks through to the URL of your choice.

Slideshow Web App. Upload Shoutlet-hosted images to create a customized slideshow web app. Each image clicks through to the URL of your choice.

Build a Digital Media Department

One day (perhaps you are here now), you'll need to operate an entire digital team. Recently, a chief marketing office (CMO) from the banking industry asked me to design a complete digital marketing organization for him. I'm providing the same plan here for you.

Chief Digital Officer (CDO) or Chief Social Officer (CSO). It's becoming more common to have a C-level executive leading the digital side of marketing. This person oversees an entire digital marketing organization and is responsible for budgeting, hiring, and business planning. This position should have a pulse on your industry and online marketing expertise with the ability to predict trends. This position leverages relationships with industry analysts to forecast a predicted positive outcome—meaning understanding that the efforts will be successful in the end. Qualified candidates should have several years' experience in leading a digital advertising agency or come from a digital platform company (Google, Facebook, etc.). This position also often plays a significant role in public relations for the company by giving speeches on the industry's digital trends.

Vice President of Online Marketing. This position focuses on implementation and management of strategic plans as directed by the company's CDO/CSO. Often this vice president is in charge of measurement, return on investment (ROI), and execution of the vision developed by the CDO/CSO.

Search Engine Optimization and Search Engine Marketing Strategist. Understanding SEO and SEM is a science. It's a job that requires continuous updating and mathematical expertise. A person in this position should be certified in Google AdWords at minimum and ideally savvy enough to keep up with the latest technologies and trends.

E-mail Service Provider (ESP). This person understands *deliverability*, the importance of *opt-in*, and *segmentation*. Like the SEO expert, this person

KEY TERMS

Deliverability The rate at which marketing messages (for example, direct mail pieces or e-mails) are delivered or undeliverable. A deliverable rate is calculated by dividing the total number of delivered messages by the total number of sent messages. An undeliverable rate is calculated by dividing the total number of messages never received by the intended recipient (undeliverables) by the total number of messages sent.

Opt-in Voluntary, trackable sign-up by recipient allowing the sender to distribute marketing e-mails to the recipient. Because of anti-spam laws, legitimate e-mail list management companies and websites require that all members of a list opt in to receive updates. This means you cannot send blanket marketing e-mails to people without first receiving their opt-in approval.

Segmentation The process of defining and subdividing a large, homogenous market into clearly identifiable segments by their similar needs, wants, or demand characteristics. The objective of segmentation is to design a marketing mix that precisely matches the customers' expectations in the targeted segment.

has perfected the craft of running e-mail campaigns by testing strategies until they yield high conversion rates.

Community Manager. This role monitors a company's blog, community, and/or social network. The manager's mission is to make sure everyone stays on message when communicating about the company's products or services and the staff is responsive to customer service needs. Unlike the social customer service person, this person focuses on general marketing, sales opportunities, and overall "happiness" of a visitor's web experience with your company.

Social Media Manager. This position concerns outbound marketing, while other roles are inward focused. This manager focuses on running marketing campaigns such as sweepstakes, coupons, or promotions. The social media manager creates awareness through external outlets. Rather than "listening" like the community manager, the social media manager "engages" by sending information outward.

Social Customer Service. This role is becoming an extension of an existing customer service department. Previously customer service dealt with issues via phone and e-mail; now these employees respond to issues on Twitter, Facebook, and Google+.

Public Relations (PR). This position is traditional in a public relations department, but this person must have a firm grasp of social media monitoring. This person continuously focuses on your brand and how it's perceived in the market. The PR person looks for opportunities to promote your company by working closely with the social media manager. The PR person focuses on the communication strategy, tone, and voice of your company, while the social media manager executes these plans.

> **ELIMINATING CROSSOVER**
>
> 
>
>
> Roles in online marketing can often be closely aligned to the point that they may overlap. Follow these tips to eliminate crossover:
>
> - Make sure the community manager does not conduct outbound social media efforts.
> - The community manager is like a hallway patrol monitor, not a content creator.

CSS/HTML Designer + Programmer. Even with the ease of use of the available social media tools, it's still necessary to have someone with web design skills on hand. I've found that most companies need constant tweaking of their Facebook apps, Twitter accounts, and online campaigns. Be prepared for these demands by having someone on your staff who can react quickly.

Online Ad Expert. This position solely focuses on display advertising. It could be combined with SEO/SEM if you find the right person. However, media buying on external sites (such as placing banner ads on the *Wall Street Journal*'s site) is a different role than bidding on Google AdWords keywords. This role needs to have traditional media buying experience, preferably coming from a print advertising, billboard, or television background. Understanding buying cycles makes a big difference when you have a budget to do display advertising. Find someone who knows these trends and understands how to measure ROI.

Social Content Manager. This position focuses on creating content for social marketing. Yes, it's a full-time job. Developing compelling video and engaging posts and contests takes time (and great content). The person in this role needs a solid background in video production, web development, and graphic design. Look for a digital content expert.

Analytics Expert. The person in this role needs a background in web analytics and familiarity with companies such as Omniture, Core Metrics, and Google Analytics. While Google Analytics is easy enough to use that an entry-level user can navigate it, a company expanding its online marketing needs someone with deeper analytics skills. This person must know how to create reports that can track a campaign from concept to conversion to sale. Find a data-driven person with a deep understanding of web measurement who knows how to use a variety of analytics tools.

Budgeting for Online Marketing

Budgets are steadily increasing in digital marketing as online options prove to be more effective and more measurable than traditional advertising options. Companies typically allot 25 percent of their overall marketing and advertising budget to online marketing. Nearly 70 percent of that online budget now goes to social media marketing.

When budgeting for online marketing, there are several factors to consider. Most people think budgeting is merely about the advertising spend. They fail to consider human resource costs, training, production, consultant fees, website hosting fees, licensing fees for social tools, and finally, the advertising spend. Now there are digital marketing calculators you can use to see where your budget should be. Visit digitalmarketing calculator.com for a quick look at what your company's budget should look like.

Building an Online Editorial/Event Calendar

The most challenging part of managing an online marketing campaign (your social media postings and blogs) is the behind-the-scenes maintenance. For most of our clients, we recommend creating an *editorial calendar* to forecast topics and *triggered events*. An editorial calendar is simple to create. All you need is a 12-month calendar (I prefer Google Calendar) and ideas.

Don't get too worried about the ideas part of creating content. It's easy if you think of your content creation and distribution as having a few different parts. For example, I always have a *main theme*, a *fixed client success story*, a *new feature announcement*, and a *recent industry trend*

Editorial calendar A schedule of the topics that you plan to cover in social media and blogs. An editorial calendar is used by bloggers, publishers, businesses, and groups to control publication of content across different media—for example, newspaper, magazine, blog, e-mail newsletters, and social media outlets like Twitter and Facebook fan pages. It is an efficient way to control publication of content across diverse media outlets over time.

Triggered events Upcoming important events and relevant events.

scheduled in my calendar. So the only variable in my content is really the industry trend. Putting that idea into practice, let's see how it works:

Area	June	July	August
Main Theme	Camping season	Holiday fireworks	Back to school
Fixed Story	Flashlights	Fire safety	Crosswalk safety
Feature	New flashlights	Lanterns	Blinking vests
Industry Trend	Solar recharging	Fuel conservation	Home schooling

Table 5-1. Major battery brand editorial calendar

You can see how quickly you can fill in blanks on your blogging or social media posting calendar. This process is an efficient way to forecast a manageable schedule of content events.

Tying Offline Efforts to Online Strategies

Several companies I've worked with have struggled to measure their offline effectiveness—in terms of actual sales or actions taken as a result of the promotions—when it comes to online marketing. I've been involved with numerous campaigns that have resulted in trackable offline sales, so I feel it's important to include some of these strategies to measure online efforts. Given the right set of tools, anything created online can be measured offline as well. It's a matter of connecting the dots.

Toll-Free Numbers

If you're conducting marketing for a company that requires an offline sale, setting up a custom toll-free number might be a good option. A cam-

TRACKABLE COUPON CODES

There are a couple ways to create trackable coupon codes that your online customers can redeem either online or in-store. Here are two services that work well for setting up your own coupons.

- RevTrax.com
- Coupons.com

CUSTOM TOLL-FREE NUMBERS

There are now tons of online services that sell custom toll-free numbers. Here are two:

- Grasshopper.com
- Vonage.com

paign manager I worked with wanted to use online marketing to reach homeowners interested in home security. If you think about it, you would not buy a home security system online. You would first need to ask a lot of questions about installation, equipment, service options, etc. Therefore the company posted a custom toll-free number at the end of online videos and in web applications to prompt a call. The online operator would close the sale, and all of it was tracked to individual web marketing efforts since it was tied to the dedicated toll-free numbers.

QR Codes

In Chapter 3, we talked about QR codes and how they tie into offline efforts. Several manufacturers have done a great job of putting QR codes on product shelves and packaging so potential customers can get additional information about the products before making a buying decision. Include a link to a mobile coupon if you try this strategy. Additionally, try to capture a visitor's e-mail address on an HTML sign-up form before giving out the coupon. Many manufacturers can only track coupon use and never really get to know their buyers. By getting their e-mail addresses or asking them to friend your Facebook page in exchange for the coupons, you can build a relationship with shoppers.

Custom URLs

You can create an online sale to generate online awareness. Create custom URLs (website links) to track your efforts. Make the URLs simple to remember so that a person can go home to make the purchase. For example, the URL coke.com/reward is easier to remember than coke.com/1245.htm.

Manager's Checklist for Chapter 5

- ☑ Begin with the end in mind. Know what success looks like before you start.
- ☑ Everyone is online. Use simple Google searches, social media monitoring tools, and relationships with professional trade associations to find them.
- ☑ Develop a digital marketing organization chart that suits your needs. If you're just beginning, a digital marketing committee is an acceptable approach.
- ☑ Determine which level your company is at when building a social media team. Examine automated processes, forming a committee, or a full organizational staff.
- ☑ Create an editorial calendar to make sure you and your team stick to a consistent schedule.
- ☑ Set up offline tracking strategies by using toll-free numbers, QR codes, and custom URLs.

External Online Engagement

What really decides consumers to buy or not to buy is the content of your advertising, not its form.

—David Ogilvy, advertising executive and author

Identifying Your Influencers

In an effort to reach your core audience online, you need to know how to find them. I have worked with several companies that have struggled to find their audience. With a couple tools and some careful planning, you can not only locate them, but also engage them and receive valuable feedback to help you perfect your campaigns. Here are a few basic ways to locate your audience.

Social Media Monitoring and Keyword Search. Conversations are already happening about your company, your products, and your services online. Many times when I walk into a prospect's office, I arrive with a complete printout of conversations about his or her company. The customer stares with amazement as he or she wonders how I ever found such conversations. It's simple. There are hundreds of free social media monitoring companies available online. Earlier I wrote about Social Mention (social mention.com) as a free service that lets you track keyword mentions and sentiment. It allows you to check in to see what others are saying about your company. Once you set up keywords about your company, you'll quickly discover where conversations are happening. Turn it up a notch and create a keyword list around activities or interests that your potential customers may share. For example, instead of searching for Solo Cup, perhaps try picnics. You'll soon have a list of several blogs, chat rooms, and social networks to filter through for key influencers. It's also important to check the quality of these conversations over the course of a couple of months. Several advertising agencies offer services to "qualify" blogs and social networks before you decide to invest in these sites or set up a marketing campaign. These agencies audit the sites to ensure that their stated visitation statistics are backed up and accurate, advertising rates are within industry standards, etc. The agencies can advise you on advertising placement. In many cases, the sites you ultimately advertise with will pay them a commission as a finder's fee (meaning you don't pay the agencies out of pocket).

Google Alerts (google.com/alerts). You can easily set up keywords via free Google Alerts, which alerts you via e-mail whenever a term is mentioned. Begin with your company, then expand into more specific keywords based on your company's activities, relevant topics, or interests. Filter the results and refine your list of locations. Then contact these websites, blogs, or social networks for an advertising media kit.

KEY TERM

Media kit A packet of electronic or print information that includes advertising details such as rates, mechanical specs, visitor demographics, and editorial calendar.

TRICKS OF THE TRADE

What If They Won't Sell to Me?

Sometimes the sites you find that hold conversations about your key topics do not accept advertising. If that is the case, be creative. See if you can provide a guest blog. Comment on their blog posts if they have this option. Or see if they might distribute your products for a commission.

Surveys. You can obtain a great deal of information from your audience by asking them the three background questions: Where are you hanging out online? What kind of content do you like to receive? How can we most effectively reach you? Most companies have access to trade associations or e-mail lists that they can use to generate quick surveys. If

> **GET SURVEYS FOR FREE**
>
> TRICKS OF THE TRADE
>
> In the early days of developing a social media strategy for clients, we often used tactics to gain valuable insights for our client's targets by partnering with bloggers and trade associations.
>
> On the business-to-consumer (B2C) projects, we would create an online survey and ask a blogger if we could partner on surveying his or her readers. Sometimes we would give away gift cards or offer to share the survey results with the bloggers so they could better understand their own audience and leverage the information for future advertising revenue.
>
> For the business-to-business (B2B) projects, we used a similar approach but partnered with industry trade associations instead of blogs. This let us get in front of the exact audience we wanted to reach, every time.

you use an online survey tool like Survey Monkey (surveymonkey.com), you can gain immediate insights from the second you send a survey to your list. Ask *open-ended questions* so you don't skew your results. Open-ended questions are designed to encourage a full, meaningful answer using the subject's own knowledge and/or feelings. Look for patterns in your findings that indicate what blogs, social networks, or online groups your audience is visiting.

Once you have identified your audience based on discussion topics and interests, you can engage them. I recall a specific campaign I was involved in for Sara Lee. The campany was launching a new product line and wanted to target people at home who enjoyed baking—not only casual bakers, but those who thought they might want to bake as a career. Using the methods discussed above, we pinpointed online audiences that hit Sara Lee's target exactly. One of the social networks we located was Bakespace.com. From our research, we found several sites that were an exact fit for semipro bakers. There was no question that the 45,000 bakers in

> **BLOGGER DISCLOSURE GUIDELINES**
>
> CAUTION
>
> The Federal Trade Commission (FTC) requires that a blogger disclose his or her relationship with your company if the blogger is receiving any compensation or reward for promoting your products or services. Follow the guidelines closely and make certain you disclose your own objectives before formalizing partnerships. Find out about these laws and regulations by visiting the FTC website (ftc.gov/opa/2009/10/endortest.shtm).

this community were seriously into baking. Once we located this audience, we set up a partnership with the site and syndicated Sara Lee–branded baking videos with the community. Since Sara Lee was promoting baking and the site targeted bakers, these videos reached a specific audience in a way that was nondisruptive to their user experience. Part of online marketing success involves locating and understanding your audience; the other part requires developing compelling content that will engage that community and be shared with like-minded people.

Garbage In, Garbage Out

In computer programming, we use the acronym *GIGO* (garbage in, garbage out), which means that what you put into your computer programming code is what you get out of it. I believe the same is true for online marketing.

A while ago, I took my three children to Walt Disney World. As I was walking around the theme park buying toys and going on rides, I realized that none of the rides or toys would exist without the Disney movies. Disney specializes in content creation. It's the films that drive us to want to buy the products and go to the parks.

Similar to Disney's strategy, look at Apple. If it hadn't made deals with all the record companies and movie studios prior to launching its famous iTunes® store, would you have purchased an iPod®? Both companies completely understand the value of content.

> SMART MANAGING
>
> **Dating Before Marriage**
>
> Unless you are part of an arranged marriage, you likely wouldn't marry before you date someone. And even in arranged marriages, each family usually vets the other party before supporting the union. Online marketing, or any marketing for that matter, is similar. You must provide value or build a relationship before you can expect a long-term commitment. Provide value before you request a sale.

Creating compelling content isn't an art form. It all comes down to understanding what type of content your audience feels is nondisruptive to their user experience. Many companies are so focused on creating an online sale, they forget about the importance of building a relationship.

Reel in your expectations until we define the steps for

creating compelling content. No one knows exactly why certain videos, tweets, or blog posts get viewed millions of times by web visitors over other pieces of content, and we may never know. Many marketing professionals are looking for ways to get as much media coverage as possible for the least production costs. My advice: don't overdo the broadcast of content in your effort to get noticed. It won't work.

> **OPTING OUT**
>
> 
>
>
> Have you ever signed up for an e-mail newsletter that interested you, only to opt out a few months later because you got too much e-mail to read—and it distracted from the personal and professional e-mails you needed to read? Consider this when you create your content. Use discretion in how often you reach your audience—and in what you send them. Creating a loyal customer base that refers you to others is more important than getting one stray sale from someone who finally responds to your ninth weekly offer of a particular product.

Over the past few years, I've worked on several online campaigns. I've found the following tactics to be most effective when creating content that gets passed on from web visitors to others.

Add value. Instead of creating product videos or commercials about your company, provide your audience with something more meaningful. When we worked on a campaign for International Trucks, we created videos about "eating healthy on the road" that were "brought to you by International Trucks." This approach gained many more video views over posting videos about their new truck models. Remember to *ask* your audience what type of content would be interesting to them before spending money producing videos, etc. Think of how you can provide value by creating content that is relevant, engaging, and nondisruptive to their user experience.

Create sound bites. I've been involved in media training over the past several years, and I've discovered how short people's attention spans are when it comes to media consumption

> **CHECK KEYWORDS**
>
> 
>
>
> Check on all your keywords before embarking on a campaign to enhance search results.

Interview Yourself

When coming up with sound bites or figuring out which content is most important to highlight, imagine you are interviewing yourself in a two-minute spot. If you had two minutes to describe your company, which questions which you want to answer? Now write those questions as if you were conducting the interview. Those are questions you want your customers to ask—and ones you want to answer for them.

and how they have been trained to think in *sound bites,* meaning short informational spurts. The best way to create sound bites is to practice. Make certain you end each paragraph of text with an actionable insight.

Watch or listen to your local newscast and notice how many times they shift topics and how quickly they move on to the next sentence. They do this to retain your attention so you won't change the channel.

Leverage trends. Piggyback your content on what's hot in the media now. Reporters love to relate stories to content they are already developing. For example, International Trucks came out with articles that were timely during the 2008 economic crisis that talked about how fuel-efficient their new models were for trucking companies. Keep up with world events and build your content around what's hot.

Make content absorption easy. Make it easy to digest the content you distribute. International Trucks knew that its audience was on the road; therefore, podcasts were the best option for their content distribution. Today, items like Infographics and iPad applications seem to be emerging trends. Information graphics, or infographics, are graphic visual representations of information, data, or knowledge. These graphics present complex information quickly and clearly, such as in signs, maps, journalism, technical writing, and education. Sometimes you can have great content but a poor distribution strategy. Take a step back and determine the best distribution methods for your company.

Develop user-generated content. Sometimes you don't know what content will work or how you'll distribute it. I've seen many examples of companies that have leveraged their audience to create content for them. Keep in mind that "no one hates his or her own baby." This means that if your audience creates it, they'll like it. Consider setting up a contest or community of your own, and encourage your audience to submit content or ideas.

Be Like Magazines

Look no farther than magazines to find strategies for soliciting content from others. Periodicals run contests and ask for reader contributions to fill their pages. You can do the same. Most people want to see their ideas published, and many don't charge for content because they want publicity, too!

Socializing Your Existing Website

It still amazes me when I talk to prospective clients how little they do to make their existing website "social." So many of these companies have great content on their pages just waiting to be shared with the world. Unfortunately, the world will never interact with their content because they are missing the essential tools to bring their sites up to the new standard of social media sharing.

The first thing I do when working with new clients is to imagine myself as a digital marketing person working in their company. This allows me to understand their resource constraints and opportunities. I examine their existing website and determine how I can make their content portable and shareable via social media tactics.

Here are several simple tactics that will work immediately if added to your site.

- **Facebook "Like" button.** Now that Facebook makes up around 80 percent of the web, meaning 80 percent of users will go to Facebook before other sites, it's important to make sure the content from your own website or blog can be quickly shared on Facebook. Have your web developer insert the "Like" button in press releases, product content information, and your home page (developers.facebook .com/docs/reference/plugins/like).
- **Twitter button.** Add the Twitter button to your site and blog. This makes it easy for people to tweet about information they find on your website (twitter.com/about/resources/buttons).
- **Google's +1 button.** Google+ is gaining traction in the market as another social site. Additionally, having a +1 button on your content can help your SEO receive a positive score since Google is still a leader in search technology (google.com/webmasters/+1/button).

- **RSS.** Several companies have news articles or press releases just sitting on their websites. Create an RSS feed web application so the news feed can be shared across the social web. Companies like mine—Shoutlet (shoutlet.com)—make it easy to create these news feed web applications.
- **Podcasts.** Like RSS, several companies have product videos, training videos, audio programs, and more on their website that cannot be shared in their current format. Podcasts are easy to set up and give you another channel for content distribution. For example, Snap-On Tools does a great job of distributing product training videos to salespeople and franchisees via podcasts.
- **Sharing Bar.** Using tools like ShareThis (sharethis.com), AddThis (addthis.com), or Shoutlet, you can quickly create sharing bars that allow you to share any of your content, web pages, or blog entries across hundreds of social networks and e-mail services. Visit one of these sites to learn how easy it is to set up a social sharing bar on your site.

TRICKS OF THE TRADE

SUBMITTING YOUR PODCAST TO THE ITUNES STORE

If users can successfully subscribe to their feed using the Advanced menu in iTunes, they're ready to submit your feed. Here's how:

1. Launch iTunes.
2. In the left navigation column, click on iTunes Store to open the store.
3. Once the store loads, go to the Podcasts page by clicking on Podcasts along the top navigation bar.
4. In the right column of the Podcasts page, click on the Submit a Podcast link.
5. Follow the instructions on the Submit a Podcast page.

Online Tools (Free and Paid)

Once social media and online marketing become your job, you'll need tools to help you manage everything. Many of the search, advertising, and analytics services we talked about in previous chapters can be managed directly on their *native platforms* (such as Google, Facebook, etc.)—meaning they are made by those companies for use on their sites. Additionally, several third-party tools have emerged to make your job easier by consolidating several of those features plus new functions not

Influence The published opinion that others have about your brand and how many users or followers of them may be influenced to think similarly.

Sentiment The positive or negative feelings a person has about your brand online. Though sentiment is a challenge to accurately measure, monitoring tools can give you a high-level view of positive or negative conversations happening about your products or company and report back this to you in the form that charts the information.

Volume The amount of "buzz" that exists about your brand. Studying spikes in buzz can help you determine if there is a triggered event—such as an advertising campaign—that you should pay attention to.

provided by the native platforms. Third-party web marketing platforms can be broken into a few categories:

Social Media Monitoring. We mentioned this tool earlier in the chapter. Use monitoring tools if you work in an environment where you're highly dependent on your brand's reputation or you work in a highly regulated industry such as banking or insurance. Retailers and manufacturers of consumer goods have less need for continued monitoring, but may find it useful from time to time when marketing to their audience on a specific social site. You have several social media monitoring tools to choose from. Prices range from several hundred thousand dollars per year down to free resources. Listed below are some of the tools companies are using:

- Radian6 (radian6.com)
- Seesmic (seesmic.com)
- Lithium (lithium.com)
- Social Mention (socialmention.com)

Social Media Marketing. This is different from monitoring. *Social media marketing* is the effort of attracting new customers using specific marketing strategies. Most companies have a need for social media marketing. Whether you are marketing to other businesses or directly to consumers, there are several ways in which social media marketing can help you succeed in reaching the people who matter most to your company.

Several social media marketing applications have emerged on the market today. Each has specific uses depending on what you hope to accomplish.

Social Media Marketing

Here are some of the tools available to assist in your social media marketing efforts.

Web apps. These applications range from RSS feed readers to sign-up forms. Web applications are ideal for engaging customers on your Facebook pages and your company website. Several web applications have sharing capabilities that allow visitors to pass along your content to their friends either via e-mail or by embedding a link onto external sites and social networks.

Contests/sweepstakes. These are an exceptional way to gather information from your audience in ways specific to your brand. While many companies rely on Facebook pages to absorb and gather information about their brand, contests can collect far more relevant information. For example, if you sell camping products, on your contest entry form, ask the contest entrants, "When is your next camping trip?" This type of information isn't collected in a Facebook profile, so it gives you greater insight that facilitates better targeting.

Facebook applications and landing pages. Social media marketing tools let you quickly create Facebook applications and website landing pages to target your audience with specific content. These pages can change dynamically based on the information collected from Facebook profiles, contests, etc.

Mobile apps. These are easy to create in some social media marketing platforms. Mobile applications enable your customers to interact with your brand on the go from their phones. Several companies use services like Foursquare to allow on-premise marketing to their customers—meaning companies can track where customers are physically and send them customized marketing information.

- Shoutlet (shoutlet.com)
- Involver (involver.com)
- Buddy Media (buddymedia.com)
- Vitrue (vitrue.com)

Advertising. This is the paid route for reaching your audience and probably most effective, since many websites and social networks reserve the best way to connect with their members using paid methods. Here are the tools that I've seen used most by agencies and clients:

- Alchemy (alchemysocial.com)
- AdParlor (adparlor.com)

- Marin Software (marinsoftware.com/products/facebook-ads)
- Qwaya (qwaya.com)

Measuring Online Return on Investment

At speaking events I'm often challenged by a marketing person about measurement. Using social media, marketing professionals are trying to determine which marketing efforts lead to which direct sales. Every action online can be tracked and measured. It's a matter of tools and resources to gain the insights you need to measure or prove an ROI (return on investment). I've found the following methods to be most valuable when it comes to ROI measurement:

Pixel tracking. If you run an e-commerce site, you can create a tracking procedure that allows you to measure a sale when the customer exits to your receipt page. Many advertising platforms do pixel tracking to measure all the way from first click on your site to checkout. If you are looking to measure social media marketing efforts, choose a vendor that offers pixel tracking. Find out how to create tracking pixels here: help.yahoo.com/l/us/yahoo/ywa/faqs/tracking/advtrack/3520294.html.

Data collection. Businesses that market to other businesses struggle to measure ROI. For most B2B companies that I have worked with, measurement is more about lead generation than a direct sale. For example, if you sell houses, it's unlikely that someone would purchase a house through an e-commerce site. Therefore, you'll want to focus on tactics that get you the lead via a sign-up form or contest so you can make a direct sale later. The right social media marketing vendor will have APIs (application programming interfaces) that enable you to track lead flow generation, which ultimately will provide an ROI for your online campaigns.

Epic Failure: What Not to Do

Online marketing is a careful balance of skill and technology. Understanding how to communicate in various social networks, blogs, and forums is critical. The following information is crucial. It could save your company from a complete public relations disaster or even worse—loss of your job. Here's a list of the top actions not to take in the world of online marketing:

- **Don't create fake personas.** Never—for any reason—create a fake Twitter, Facebook, or blog account to use for anonymous marketing purposes. I've seen big companies banned from Facebook and Google when they created phony accounts to appear to be a customer promoting the company's products and services.
- **Don't oversell.** So many online marketing people want to get directly to the sale so they overdo it. It's really easy to turn people off by pushing too many sales messages to them, especially on social networks. Reserve your direct response strategies for paid advertising and e-mail marketing where offers are generally more acceptable. Remember that social media is about building a relationship with your audience first and the sale comes second.
- **Don't react negatively online.** It's far too easy to immediately tweet back to someone who may be slamming your products on Twitter, etc. Always use a professional tone when responding to negativity online. Remember, the web is forever and it's hard to undo any heated discussion you get yourself into. Instead of arguing online, you can offer a number for the complainer to call and take the conversation offline. I've found that people are bolder online than they are on the phone or in person. Use offline interactions to your advantage.
- **Don't ignore people.** Once you commit to social media, as I mentioned earlier in the book, you must respond to questions and issues. People are impatient online, so make sure you respond quickly. A one-hour response time is ideal, but you must respond within one day. Social media monitoring tools keep these issues manageable for you.

SMART MANAGING

What to Do with Negative Press

In the name of being authentic, some businesses now welcome even some negative comments from customers. For example, a professional speaker who included a list of *all* audience reviews from a particular event—including one from a heckler—in his press kit might be taken more seriously than one who handpicks and publishes only the best comments from his last 100 speeches. If handled properly, such disclosure gives the customer a chance to see you authentically. This actually can strengthen your reputation. If you publish negative comments or press, be cautious in how you do it.

TRICKS OF THE TRADE

SOCIAL MEDIA MONITORING TOOLS

HootSuite is a social media management system for businesses and organizations to collaboratively execute campaigns across multiple social networks from one secure, web-based dashboard. Launch marketing campaigns, identify and grow audience, and distribute targeted messages using HootSuite's unique social media dashboard. Streamline team workflow with scheduling and assignment tools and reach audiences with geo-targeting functionality. Invite multiple collaborators to manage social profiles securely, plus provide custom reports using the comprehensive social analytics tools for measurement. Key social network integrations include Facebook, Twitter, LinkedIn, and Google+ Pages, plus a suite of social content apps for YouTube, Flickr, Tumblr, and more. To learn more, visit hootsuite.com.

Engaging customers online may seem monumental, but with the tools in this chapter, you should have a clearer idea how to reach them using targeted apps and strategies. Find them and engage them with compelling content and service.

Manager's Checklist for Chapter 6

- ☑ The best way to find where your audience is online is to ask them through a survey.
- ☑ Partner with trade associations to get survey feedback quickly and often for free.
- ☑ Make sure you post content that is valuable and nondisruptive to a user's experience on social networks. Don't always push for the sale; build a relationship first.
- ☑ Use social media marketing tools and a monitoring platform to manage your routine marketing tasks.
- ☑ Set up tracking pixels and APIs to track direct ROI.
- ☑ Stay alert when communicating online. Remember, the web makes conversations permanent.

Internal Online Engagement

You can have brilliant ideas, but if you can't get them across, your ideas won't get you anywhere.

—Lee Iacocca, former president/CEO, Chrysler Motors

Internal communication is a problem for many companies, and the bigger you grow, the larger the issue becomes. Employees are constantly seeking information and grow frustrated if there is no source for answers. One solution companies look to for resolving this issue is a company intranet. Intranets are important because they provide a central location to store internal company information and to communicate with staff. The key advantages to an intranet are easy access, inexpensive implementation and maintenance, improved information sharing, scalability, and flexibility.

Some of the key benefits of intranets include:

- **Better internal communications.** Corporate information can be stored and accessed at any time.
- **More effective resource sharing and best practices.** A virtual community can be created to facilitate information sharing and collaborative work.
- **Improved customer service.** Better access to accurate and consistent information by your staff leads to enhanced levels of customer service.

KEY TERM

Intranet An internal network where an organization's information can be shared with employees and others the company gives access to, for example, the board of directors.

- **Reduction in paperwork.** Forms can be accessed and completed on the desktop, then forwarded for approval, without ever having to be printed, and with the benefit of an audit trail.
- **Increased employee awareness and engagement.** Employees who are better informed and able to communicate are more apt to be engaged in their projects and workplace.
- **Improved project management.** Projects that are tracked from a centralized dashboard are easier for multiple employees to access, update, and follow.

Effective intranets become integrated into users' everyday tasks, making the job of every employee easier. If your employees aren't using an intranet daily or at least weekly, then it either is not offering the proper information and tools or it is not serving employees productively.

FOR EXAMPLE

INTRANET DEFICIENCY

A 2009 survey by Forrester Research showed that only 43 percent of enterprise employees access an intranet daily. Worse, another 35 percent doesn't even use the intranet on a monthly basis.

The intranet needs to be turned into an *information broker platform,* meaning a location where information is freely and easily created, aggregated, shared, and accessed with minimal effort by the users. Such an intranet gives everybody access to all available information and has enough room for virtually infinite amounts of information.

SMART MANAGING

SAVE YOURSELF TIME—GET AN INTRANET

An intranet system might take time to set up on the front end, but you will save your organization time—and likely money—in the long run. For example, an intranet can help with employee orientation by providing a central source of archived content to speed the training process. Make key information accessible for employees so they can easily educate themselves and increase their effectiveness.

Intranet in a Virtual Setting

You might think that an intranet isn't useful in a virtual setting, but the opposite is true: it's imperative. You need a place where you can post information, share it, discuss it, and even edit and repost it. Communication in a virtual setting becomes more electronic-dependent than in a traditional setting. An intranet is a very effective way to ensure that employees are working together toward the same goals and vision.

You may have heard of something being "in the cloud." Cloud computing is the use of computing resources (hardware and software) that are delivered as a service over a network (typically the Internet). Many companies offer cloud-based data storage services. The name comes from the use of a cloud-shaped symbol as an abstraction for the complex infrastructure it contains in system diagrams. Cloud computing entrusts remote services with a user's data, software, and computation. Intranets are a form of cloud computing that provide marketing materials, file sharing, human resource information, training and sales materials, company calendars, etc.

Setting Up a Company Intranet

Setting up a company intranet takes time and planning. You first need to establish goals for your intranet: What are you looking to accomplish? Are you trying to train staff on new releases? Create an FAQ section? Improve communications throughout the company? Do you plan to include all company departments on the intranet or only certain departments? Who will manage the intranet and be charged with updating content? Establishing the intranet goals determines what types of information are needed and in the end determines the organization. Next, you need to think about timing. When do you want to go live? Timing is a big factor in choosing the right solution for your company. You also need to consider a budget. How much are you willing to spend on internal communication? Many organizations will build an intranet to fit your exact company needs, but this also comes with a price tag.

Once you have determined your goals, you need to research intranet providers or decide if you're going to build your own in-house solution.

Determine Your Intranet Goals

Before you create your intranet, determine the goals you have for its use. Your business's efficiency can be improved by using your intranet for some of these purposes:

- **Publishing**—delivering information and business news
- **Document management**—viewing, printing, and working collaboratively on office documents
- **Training**—accessing and delivering various types of e-learning to a user's desktop
- **Workflow**—managing administrative processes
- **Front-end to corporate systems**—providing a common interface for corporate databases and business information systems
- **E-mail**—integrating intranet content with e-mail services

If you're going to seek help to build the intranet, there are many great intranet services providers; you just need to find the best solution for you. You need to find intranet providers whose services fit your needs.

TRICKS OF THE TRADE

Take Your Time

If you plan to build an intranet in-house, consider the time and resources it will demand from several departments. The research time can take a few weeks, even months to accomplish.

During the research phase, take note of the sections, departments, categories, and intranet layouts you like. Then, while the intranet is being built and implemented, you begin gathering the materials for each section.

Once you have selected your solution and it has been built, you add the content. Here's where you review your goals and see who's going to manage the intranet. This person will need to add content to the relevant sections or work with managers to show them how to upload content. Not only will you need to create training or documentation on how to add content to the intranet, but you may also need to create training materials to teach the staff how to use the intranet. You have spent a lot of time building

TRICKS OF THE TRADE

Try Before You Buy

You will learn a lot about a provider's ability to meet your needs if you sit through product demos and even go through a demo phase that applies the product to your situation.

Key Questions to Ask

Before you set up your intranet, ask yourself these key questions:

- What are my goals for the intranet?
- What key features do I need?
- Who needs to provide input on its setup?
- Who will have access, and who won't?
- How do I want it to look and feel?
- What level of technical capability will its users have?
- What is my budget for this project?

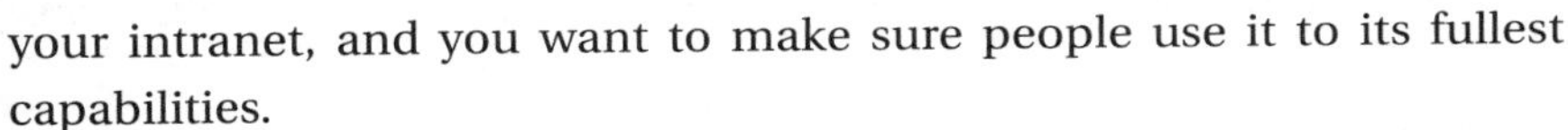

your intranet, and you want to make sure people use it to its fullest capabilities.

Once your intranet is live, you must continuously remind staff that it is there and encourage them to use it. You can send out periodic friendly e-mail reminders, or if you hear staff asking each other questions, you can refer them to the intranet. For new employees, you can introduce them to the intranet during their orientation. Most important, you want to ensure the content is always up-to-date, relevant, and easy to find. If information isn't updated, it will only break down the companywide communication. Appoint a manager for each section and give him or her the responsibility and authority to ensure his or her share of the content

Give Your Intranet a Different Face

TRICKS OF THE TRADE

It is a good idea to give your intranet a different image and structure from your customer-facing website. This will help to give your internal communications their own identity and prevent employees from confusing internal and external information.

Intranet Resources

Intranets come in many varieties. Here are some resources for building yours:

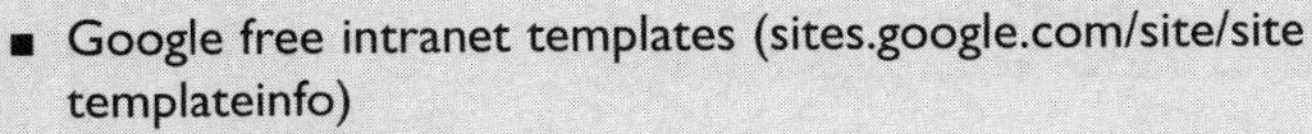

- Google free intranet templates (sites.google.com/site/site templateinfo)
- Huddle (huddle.com)
- Igloo (igloosoftware.com)
- Intranet Dashboard (intranetdashboard.com)

is always up-to-date. Remember: this is your company resource center, and it exists to facilitate internal communications.

Developing an Online Media Room

An *online media room* incorporates information that tells staff or those outside the organization what the business is about, what it is currently doing, and other relevant news. An online media room may be available on the intranet for employees only or on the Internet for the public. Typical items included on an intranet might include:

- Basic information, e.g., business overview, business lines, office addresses, etc.
- Corporate governance, e.g., mission statement and strategy, annual reports, organization chart, senior management team, corporate policies, etc.
- Corporate communications, e.g., press releases, internal news, etc.
- Case studies, white papers, research, and articles about your company.

The basis of any media room is simple. Make your content accessible, easy to share, and easy to view. Think about the type of information requests you typically receive from reporters and ensure that all that information is readily available to employees so they can answer questions.

You may choose to make this same media room available to the public, or you may create a separate media room for this purpose. Your public-facing media room may contain some of the same documents, but its content should be geared less for internal operations procedures and more for general marketing of the organization. The sidebar offers some tips for creating a strong public media room.

SMART

MANAGING

ELEMENTS OF A MEDIA ROOM

When creating your press release archive, think about how far back your audience may be looking, and determine what categories make the most sense for your news.

Some useful items to add to an online newsroom include:

- High resolution photos, logos
- Executive bios
- RSS feeds
- Corporate backgrounders

TRICKS OF THE TRADE

Online Media Room

Here are some tips for creating a useful public-facing media room:

- **Make your online media room easy for web browsers to find.** Several companies bury their media rooms under the About Us pages in their websites. Make sure you call out on your home page where your media room can be found and create a direct link to it.
- **Avoid passwords.** It's too easy to bury your logos and corporate videos behind a password-protected site. Most of your content can easily be found online anyway, so anything public-facing should be accessible on a non-password-protected page. You can get even more mileage with your media and public relations content if you post it using a wire service, such as PR Newswire (www.prnewswire.com) or Businesswire (www.businesswire.com). Through those two services, you pay to distribute a press release (cost depends on the reach and distribution list) to the media via the two websites. Use of content sharing sites like Slideshare (www.slideshare.com) and YouTube (www.youtube.com) can also help your content get out there.
- **Make contact information easy to find.** Be sure your contact information is prominently placed on every press release or media clip, even if it's already on your website. Most media professionals don't have time to look up your information. Additionally, you should add LinkedIn (www.linkedin.com) connections so media professionals can easily build a relationship with your media team.
- **Incorporate SEO.** Just as you have worked on your other pages for search engine optimization, make sure your media room has the appropriate tags, keywords, and metadata to be picked up by major search engines. Refer to Chapter 2 for specific SEO tactics.

Measuring Internal Engagement

There are several ways to measure *internal engagement*—that is, how your intranet is accessed and used. The first option is usage statistics. See if your intranet service has tracking tools to assemble monthly activity reports to see how often pages are accessed and whether content is viewed and downloaded. The second way to measure internal engagement is through user feedback. It may be easy to overhear informal feedback about the intranet, but the way to gauge feedback effectively is to survey users about their experience with the intranet. Next is metrics; depending on the goals for the intranet, the metrics could measure different things. For example, metrics can measure the success of a social media account or campaign. Engagement tracking tools can monitor the fan engagement and interaction on the page.

Sync Your Intranet Objectives with Your Corporate Strategy

An intranet has to be aligned to the corporate strategy because it is probably one of the few applications accessible to and used by every employee. Often there are at least a dozen major risks, such as losing key staff, failing to fulfill compliance requirements, and delays in releasing new products.

> SMART MANAGING
>
> 
>
> **MANAGING THE GATEWAYS OF COMMUNICATION**
>
> Distributing information through an intranet ensures consistent and controlled communication across the company. Intranets can have various levels of access based on employees' position in the company. Employees can have access to or be locked out of specific information.

Many risks can be reduced significantly through an effective intranet. The board of directors has a duty to the shareholders to reduce operational risks. All intranet managers should have the corporate risk manager as their best friend, because the risk manager usually reports directly to the board and can be an important advocate for the intranet (cmswire.com/cms/enterprise-20/the-importance-of-aligning-corporate-intranet-strategies-010820.php).

Making Intranets Relevant

Intranets will fail if the content is not relevant to employees. That is why we emphasize the importance of keeping content up-to-date and relevant. There is nothing worse than sales reps using outdated marketing materials or staff being trained on old material.

According to surveys, many intranets suffer from a lethal "trifecta" of ineffectiveness:

1. Outdated information
2. Ineffective tools for employee collaboration
3. Poor organization and lousy search engine capabilities

The unpredictable nature of knowledge work is why we need to give knowledge workers access to all relevant information. Since we don't know what might be relevant until a specific need arises (which we might be unaware of until we discover certain information), we can't really put the currently relevant information in one "for keeps" pile and all other information in a to-be-trashed pile. What's unnecessary today might be important tomorrow.

We also need to provide employees with tools so they can create or capture information to share with each other, to increase the odds that they can access enough information to serve their needs.

MAKE IT ACCESSIBLE SMART MANAGING

Think back to the earlier chapters when we discussed building a community of online evangelists who are eager to share information about your company. The same concept applies within the workplace. Make the information on your intranet easily accessible and shareable by employees within your network—so they can engage and teach others.

To help employees locate information relevant to their tasks when they need it, we need to create powerful *pull mechanisms* that bring relevant information to the surface and place it at the fingertips of your employees exactly when they need it.

Pull mechanism Accessibility points where a user can request the transmission of information.

A major reason that intranets fail today's knowledge workers (employees) is that the information they provide is still produced with a *push-based production model.* This model assumes that all information resources on the intranet must be produced in advance (only serving information needs that can be anticipated) by a small subset of all available resources (employees) and that the entire body of information must be supervised by a few people who control the message, format, and/or organization of the information resources. Such an attitude produces an intranet that is rarely up-to-date.

A cutting-edge intranet can pull in information from social media and RSS feeds through external resources like the *New York Times,* making it an automated inbound news hub. The social intranet, for example, is a pull platform with mechanisms for automatically attracting relevant information and people to you.

LIMIT OPTIONS

While it's important to include all relevant information for employees, listing too many options can decrease performance and create stress. Information abundance does not equal an abundance of choice. Deliver targeted content, and your users will not get overwhelmed. This is why a pull method works best—it delivers only the user-relevant content.

Manager's Checklist for Chapter 7

- ☑ The bigger the company, the more important internal communications become. Corporate intranets should be accessible and practical.
- ☑ List your internal communication goals before searching for an intranet platform. Platform features vary based on need.
- ☑ Online media rooms can be used both internally and externally for communicating with employees or media professionals.
- ☑ Content is key in making intranets effective. Make sure your internal content stays as fresh as your external marketing content.

Social Commerce

Middle-class people sit around trying to think of how to spend money. One of the most powerful ways to figure that out is looking at what your friends are buying, people you trust.

—Andrew Mason, founder of Groupon

Social commerce is an extension of e-commerce in which selling relies on people sharing products and services with their friends via social networks. Over the past few years, an entire industry has been built around companies looking to capitalize on friendships. There are various approaches to social commerce, since each social network operates differently. For example, Twitter has a limited number of characters you can post when promoting items for sale, so your tactics are limited compared to listing products on Facebook.

Making a Sale Using Social Commerce

Facebook commerce, also known as *F-commerce*, is the process by which companies sell their products or services on Facebook. There are two approaches to selling on Facebook. You can either choose a software platform that enables you to sell your products directly on Facebook, or you can list your product information (price, description, quantity, etc.) and offer a link to your e-commerce site for the transaction or sale to take place on your company site.

F-Commerce Platforms

Below are several F-commerce platforms you can use to facilitate sales on Facebook:

- Social Shop 2 (bigcommerce.com/socialshop2)
- Payvment (payvment.com)
- ShopTab (shoptab.net)
- Wishpond (corp.wishpond.com/social-store)
- TabJuice (tabjuice.com)
- Beetailer (beetailer.com)

F-Marketing Expenses

You don't need to spend thousands of dollars to sell your products and/or services on Facebook. Most companies have already invested money in e-commerce solutions and would prefer not to pay double transaction fees to sell their products on Facebook. Instead of using an F-commerce solution, use a *social media marketing platform* that lets you list your products on Facebook but links back to your existing e-commerce site for the sale. These strategies allow you to keep your transaction costs lower and avoid duplicate investments.

T-commerce is the process of selling your products and/or services through Twitter. Twitter is more challenging than Facebook for selling products since tweets are not visible for very long, unlike a Facebook app. Regardless, several companies have done well selling on Twitter. The best approach to selling on Twitter is to have a *flash sale,* a sale with a strong discount, a limited-time offer (most flash sales are under an hour), or a promotion of your products using Twitter but referring back to your e-commerce page or Facebook app that contains your product listing. For example, you might tweet, "We just launched our most exciting line of athletic shoes ever. Check out our limited supply here [link to your product line]."

Selling on Twitter isn't difficult. Just make certain you follow the strategies and tactics outlined in the previous chapters before beginning. When selling on Twitter, remember these tips:

- Be sure your Twitter profile is complete and explains your company and what it offers.
- Don't sell continuously; offer value to your customers. It's okay to have a Twitter account for sales only if it's clear to your followers that the site is for sales (i.e., Dell's Outlet offering discount products).

- Ensure your tweets contain keywords that can be found in your SEO algorithms. You do this by being specific when you mention a product or service in your tweets.
- Use analytics tools (Omniture, Google Analytics) that let you tag your tweets so you can track your marketing efforts from the original post through to the sale.

Dell and Twitter

FOR EXAMPLE

Dell Outlet uses Twitter for posting its Outlet products to the public. Dell only offers products on its Twitter account a few days per week to avoid overselling to its audience. Dell also uses tracking URLs (unique links for each promotion that allow them to measure response received) to determine which products are most popular. According to online sources, Dell Outlet has booked more than $3 million in revenue that can be attributed to its Twitter posts.

There is no silver bullet when selling through social media, so it's important that you focus your efforts on several tactics until you discover which tactics are most effective for your company. Most social media strategists agree that there are six Cs to remember when selling by social media. Follow these six Cs when planning your social media program:

1. **Content.** Keep in mind that search engines such as Google continuously crawl web content and reward companies that keep their websites, social networks, and blogs fresh and engaging. Provide something of value beyond offers.
2. **Community.** Approach your audience with meaningful *points of connection.* Speak to them as if they are your friends. People talk to other people online, so be sure to ask them to invite others to join your online family.
3. **Commerce.** Even though we discuss the importance of not overselling several times in this book, have enough common sense to *always* link to a path to buy your products or services. You can start entire e-commerce sites quickly and inexpensively these days, so always list your products for sale online. If you sell through retailers or other business partnerships, point your social media followers to those sites.
4. **Context.** In today's world you have companies like Foursquare that help you be creative in how you communicate with your audience. If

you know they are checking into one of your retail stores, reward them for visiting stores/locations in person (rather than online shopping, for example). Adjust your communication style as needed to address a direct audience—meaning the people or customers you are trying to reach.

5. **Connection.** Continuing relationships after you've run a big promotion or sold directly to a customer is vital. Consider using a *social customer relationship management* (CRM) platform that will help you evaluate relationships over time and help you create more targeted campaigns as your connections grow.

> KEY TERM
>
> **CRM** A *customer relationship management* platform that helps you manage your company's interactions with customers and potential sales prospects while organizing and automating one-to-one relationships via social networks.

6. **Conversation.** Evaluating online conversations is important for understanding what is being said online about your company, products, or services. You want to make sure that you have a handle on any negative feedback about your products. The best strategy is to approach negativity and address issues before they amplify onto the social web.

> **SOCIAL COMMERCE**
>
> 
>
> TOOLS
>
> Social commerce is the use of social network(s) in the context of e-commerce transactions. Here are some sites to explore to implement your company's social commerce initiatives:
>
> - venpop.com
> - lyst.com
> - thefancy.com
> - 8thbridge.com
> - bazaarvoice.com

Attracting Two Types of Leads with Social Media

Social media is no longer an extra for business. According to Gartner, Inc., by 2014 social networking services will replace e-mail as the primary vehicle for interpersonal communications for 20 percent of business users.

Most of the success in social media is the result of careful planning and hard work. Typically it takes three to six months for your sales to get under way if you are undertaking a social strategy for the first time. Like real life, relationships must be cultivated for a while to build trust. There are two social media lead types that are important for companies to capitalize on: direct sale and influencer sale.

Direct Sale. Like the Dell example earlier, it is possible to go directly to an audience with an offer; however, this only works if you have an established brand. How effective would it be if a new computer company started with a Twitter outlet store with zero followers? As an established brand, Dell can afford to go directly to Twitter because much of the world already knows the company and is already looking for deals.

If you are starting from zero in your branding, you must first build an audience of followers. Begin by following other people who share interests similar to your potential audience's. For example, if you are a new computer company, you might begin by following Dell, then following its followers. By doing a simple Twitter search for "Dell" on Twitter's search engine, you can find trending topics, hashtags, or keywords around the brand name and follow those people who are posting messages. Many times when you begin to follow someone, he or she will reciprocate the gesture and begin to follow you. Therefore, make your Twitter bio as informative as possible with a direct link to your public website or e-commerce store in your user bio. Make sure your content is compelling enough to keep followers' attention, or they will find other companies to follow. Don't oversell them in the beginning. Be their friend. Strategies for a direct sale include:

- **Link tracking.** Make sure you create URLs that can be tracked using an analytics platform. Use a *link shortener* (bit.ly) so that you have more room for text. Link shorteners are tools that shorten URL hyperlinks (do this through a website, or through your social media management platform). Don't publicize that you use a link shortener, just make your links shorter to fit more text in your tweets.
- **Focus your messaging on immediacy.** Create messaging around Limited Time or Exclusive Offer for Our Followers. This rewards people for following your company.

> SMART MANAGING
>
> 
>
> **Understanding Influencers**
>
> *Influence* is the ability to drive action, such as sharing a picture that triggers comments and likes or tweeting about a great restaurant that causes your followers to try it for themselves. Your friends/fans (people who engage with your profile by following it) can become influencers if people respond to their posts.

Influencer Sale. This type of sale involves selling indirectly through friends. Influencers may be potential buyers themselves, or they may be "influenced" by a friend to purchase. Influencer selling is a more complex model, but provides a greater impact if you can nail it. The concept is to get a large audience excited about your products and services over a longer time.

When selling through influencers, consider these suggestions:

- **Use a coupon engine** like Coupons.com to track *pass-through referrals*—that is, the responses that come through your influencers' referrals.
- **Use a social CRM platform** to track influencers over a period of time—rather than through a single promotion.
- **Use affiliate networks** like Commission Junction (cj.com) or ClickBank (clickbank.com) to create offers and track your affiliates.
- **Use monitor influencer services** like Klout (klout.com) to stay on top of changing influencer algorithms.

Tying Your Impact to Sales

Generally, social media shouldn't be expected to directly lead to increased sales. Instead, it generates leads and conversions. If you think about revenue as a relationship and not simply a transaction, as suggested by Richard Binhammer of Dell, then you'll see that social media can have a tremendous influence on the long-term relationship.

There are two types of measurement, tangible and intangible. Tangible measurement is the easy stuff to measure when determining if your campaign is working. *Tangible measures* include transactions (sales), e-mails collected, contest sign-ups, etc. *Intangible measurements* are more difficult to measure but include items such as overall brand awareness, positive brand influence, residual sales, and product feedback. Both the measurements are valuable, and both can be tracked.

Link Shorteners

SMART MANAGING

There are several benefits in using a URL shortener. In addition to allowing you more room when it comes to a posting Twitter's limited 140 characters, shorteners provide powerful reporting and tracking options for you to see where every click is coming from. Often URL shorteners go beyond the tracking capabilities that come with Facebook's or Twitter's standard tools.

There are plenty of free link shortener tools. Register on the link shortener site, then create tracking links to track everyone who interacts with your messages. Link shortener sites include:

- Bit.ly (bitly)
- Tiny.url (tiny.url)
- goo.gl (goo.gl)

Finding Influencers

TOOLS

There are several free tools to help find your influencers online. In addition to the tools mentioned in previous chapters, you may want to try one or several of these tools:

- **Addict-o-Matic** (addictomatic.com) produces a page with consolidated search matches across blogs, Twitter, Digg, Flickr, and more.
- **Alltop** (alltop.com) is the *online magazine rack* of blogs, or a way to store all your favorite blogs in one "rack" or location. Search for influential bloggers listed by specific subject and topics.
- **Blogpulse** (nmincite.com) is an automated *trend discovery system* for blogs. It analyzes and reports on daily activity in the blogosphere so you have information on the types of topics that are generating activity.
- **Boardreader** (boardreader.com) is a search engine for forums. Get fast and quality searches for your own forum. This tool connects online communities via their keyword searches.
- **Buzzstream** (www.buzzstream.com) helps you build a dossier about your influencers. For example, you can gather information about the grade of your Twitter profile including:
  - Number of followers
  - Power of followers
  - Updates: more updates generally lead to a higher grade
  - Follower/following ratio
  - Engagement
- **Dailylife** (daylife.com) searches news and editorial commentary for influencers in traditional media.
- **HubSpot Twitter Grader** (tweet.grader.com) checks the power of a Twitter profile—meaning its influence, impact, and reach—compared to

millions of others that have been graded.

- **IceRocket** (icerocket.com) searches social networking sites and blogs to find influencers and *online creators* (people who upload images or talk passionately on a social network about a brand).
- **Klout** (klout.com) is currently the most respected measure of Twitter influence. Klout allows users to track the impact of opinions, links, and recommendations. You can track both your own impact and that of others.
- **Lijit** (lijit.com) builds relationships with online influencers and connects directly to their audiences.
- **Monitter** (monitter.com) monitors Twitter for keywords, phrases, and topics that are being discussed online.
- **PeerIndex** (peerindex.com) helps you discover the authorities and opinion formers on a given topic.
- **Technorati** (technorati.com) is considered to be the leading blog search engine, useful for finding influential blogs.
- **Twitalyzer** (twitalyzer.com) is a Twitter-focused tool that looks at influence, impact, and engagement.

FOR EXAMPLE

FROM CURIOSITY TO NECESSITY

When I began my career in social media, several clients weren't really concerned with selling through social media. Most of the time a CEO would find that a son or daughter was using Facebook, so this CEO would decide that it's the future of online marketing, and it's necessary to start immediately. So the goal in the early days for implementing social media was to simply build friends/fans/followers. Fast-forward to today, and those goals have changed. Now companies are focused on the bottom line. If social media can improve the bottom line, it holds value for those CEOs.

Some important things to understand are the impact of social media on: (1) purchase behavior, (2) search results, and (3) customer loyalty. To measure these types of functions, you need some tools.

Make sure you invest in platforms if you plan to scale your campaigns down to tangible and intangible measurements.

Deploying Your Evangelists

Activating influencers or evangelists is a marketing professional's biggest goal. Once you figure out how to turn customers into independent mar-

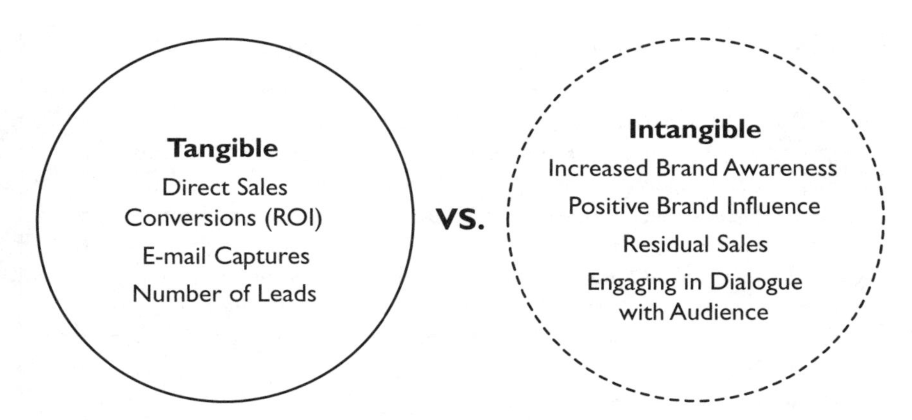

Figure 8-1. Tangible vs. intangible measurements

keters of your company, you win. The term *evangelist* is used in online marketing to refer to someone who is willing to promote your products and services even if he or she does not buy. Turning casual website visitors, Facebook fans, and Twitter followers into evangelists is a tricky task, but it can be done by following some simple rules.

> **TRACKING CUSTOMER BEHAVIOR**
>
> TOOLS
>
> Purchase behavior can be tracked through analytics platforms (Omniture, Google, CoreMetrics). Search results can be measured using various free tools from Google, Facebook, and Twitter. Customer loyalty can, over time, be measured by frequent sales tracking, social CRM and influencer tracking, and affiliate program tracking.

Talk like your customers talk. Ask yourself if you would want the content that you're producing to appear on your Facebook timeline or in your e-mail box. Observe your customers on external social sites for a few weeks before engaging them. Model their behaviors in your communication to them. If your customers speak like a teenager, make sure your marketing person can speak the same way. Potential customers are attracted to companies that remind them of themselves.

Refine your data points. Social media allows people to express themselves freely. Start your campaigns with very few data points (name, e-mail, etc.). Then rerun contests and promotions with the same audience to extend your data points. The more people trust you, the more informa-

Which Voice Is That?

Writers often talk about *voice* to refer to the tone or style of a particular author. Writers try to make their voice sound authentic and distinguishable from others. The goal in developing voice is to become more powerful and believable as an author. Voice applies to social media, too—but in regard to engaging customers. Use a voice that is compatible with your customers' and their needs. For example, if you are selling funeral services, you likely would not want to use an over-the-top, comedic "voice" in your posts. If you are selling acne cream to teenagers, you don't want to come across with the voice of a biomedical engineer. Match your voice to your audience and its needs. If you struggle with speaking in a voice that matches the needs of your target customers, hire a writer to give you tips or entries to get you started.

tion they will give you about themselves. Once you have more data, you can pinpoint their interests for future marketing campaigns.

Hang out where your customers hang out. Your customers are already spending time on social sites talking to their peers. Before encouraging these customers to visit your site and Facebook page, participate in their environment by hanging out on their turf. Build engaging dialogue that is nondisruptive to their user experience.

Don't overwhelm yourself. It's okay to take baby steps with your social program. Regardless of what agencies and social consultants tell you, it's okay to start small. Begin by linking to your archived e-mail newsletters and tweeting those pieces a couple of times per week. Add your company events to your Facebook timeline. You'll find after a short time that you'll acquire fans and followers.

Leveraging Your Existing Digital Investments

Most companies that I encounter have already invested a substantial amount of money in their marketing and e-commerce tools. Gartner, Inc. predicts that by 2017, CMOs (chief marketing officers) will outspend CIOs (chief information officers). The number of platforms you have in your marketing arsenal will increase rapidly over the next several years. To keep on top of all these moving parts, it is important to invest in technology that is flexible enough to grow with your needs.

If a *social media management system* (SMMS) is a tool your company could benefit from, the next step is embarking on the vetting process. Before you begin, identify what you need. Remember that tools should be among the final decisions you make when you're embarking on your social media program. If you have not gone through the process of solidifying your goals and mapping out your strategic plan, you risk choosing a tool that does not meet all your needs. Because social software becomes a linchpin in your social media program once it is adopted, this is a choice with long-term implications. Getting it right the first time is critical.

> **WHY MARKETING ISN'T DEAD**
>
> CAUTION
>
> I've read articles that say marketing is dead. When budgets are cut, CEOs may look around and see that their traditional advertising isn't working. I argue this point: Marketing isn't dead; it's just changing. Today, marketing is more about customer engagement than about customer bombardment. Social media and online marketing provide the optimal platforms to make this happen.

Your company's SMMS requirements (social media strategies to protect your brand) are as individual as your social media programs. Knowing what you need (and why) not only protects you from being hypnotized by glitzy features, it also helps you build a case for the expense. Knowing where you want to go with your social media program allows you to align goals with strategies, tactics, and finally, tools.

Think about the kinks in your day-to-day work, then think about what the future holds for your program. Identify what problems your company has on a day-to-day basis; eliminating these will have the most impact immediately. For example, your pain point may be that you don't have enough staff currently trained in how to create a successful social media program. This needs to be addressed. Then, think about how your social program will evolve over the next 6 to 12 months. While it's impossible to know exactly how social media will evolve over such a long time, knowing that your company wants to expand its team or launch social media in more countries, for instance, will help you scope out must-have items.

In addition to asking important questions about features, investigate pricing, training, and support. Have a ballpark price range in mind, but be flexible if your requirements point you to an SMMS that costs more. The extra expense could be worth the effort in saved time and custom development costs.

Are your team members savvy when it comes to learning new platforms? Would formal training or on-demand training (or both) suit your group?

Lastly, does your platform integrate into your existing platforms? Focus on platforms that provide a robust architecture so you can plug in and expand when the time is right. Often companies get hooked on a feature-rich system with no API connectivity—that is, the code architecture behind the platform—so it prohibits expansion down the road.

SMART

MANAGING

Why Training and Support Matter

A good training program means you will maximize the benefits of the tool because you have a full understanding of its functionality.

Like training, robust support helps your team to get the most value from its SMMS. Does the platform offer free technical support, as well as integration and strategy support? Viewing your SMMS vendor as a partner means working with the vendor regularly to pinpoint ways to leverage platform features, which increases value.

Manager's Checklist for Chapter 8

- Social commerce is an extension of e-commerce, in which selling relies on people sharing their thoughts about products and services with their friends throughout various social networks.
- To avoid double transaction fees, don't invest too heavily in social commerce platforms. Instead, look for ways to list your products and link back to your existing e-commerce site.
- There are both tangible and intangible forms of measurement. Put tools in place so you can measure both.
- Investigate platforms carefully before you purchase one. Focus on platforms that provide expansion through API connections.

Effective Tactics Based on Business Type

In real life, strategy is actually very straightforward. You pick a general direction and implement like hell.

—Jack Welch

When I give a speech about using social media to sell products, I'm often challenged by an audience member about his or her specific market and asked to give strategies that will work for that company. I break up the approaches into three categories:

1. Direct to consumer (B2C)
2. Business-to-business (B2B)
3. Nonprofit

Most people can get their minds around selling consumer products online, but several struggle with B2B and nonprofit. Yes, social media can work for any business or organization. Most organizations or businesses fail because they equate social media with Facebook. There is an entire world beyond Facebook—blogs, other social networks, mobile networks, and other direct marketing approaches. Companies also fail because they don't truly understand their audience.

Business-to-Consumer Marketing

Marketing to a business-to-consumer (B2C) audience is easier than business-to-business (B2B). However, both can be social media effective. But even B2C companies can find online marketing a challenge, depending on their product or company popularity. For example: you work for a toilet paper company and want to use social media. How exciting would your content be? If you're not selling passion products, like a Harley-Davidson, then it's going to be more challenging to keep your audience engaged.

I have several nuggets of advice for companies that want to achieve positive social media ROI and constantly improve the impact they are having on their business as a whole. Here are five critical steps to ensure your social ROI stays in the black:

1. **Remember what ROI really is.** It's easy to get caught up in metrics—fans, followers, subscribers, etc. But keep in mind that ROI is more than that. As companies dig deeper, it comes down to one thing: sales.
2. **Set your goals; then chart your path.** Know what positive ROI looks like and establish your social media goals before designing a program. This will help you build your social media program the right way from the get-go. Start with your goal in mind and work backward.
3. **Integrate and prosper.** Make sure you're taking a holistic view of your marketing plans, and integrate your traditional marketing with your social media marketing so they support each other. I'd like to say that social media is all you need, but it is only one part of your overall marketing mix. Social media is one channel, but not the only one.
4. **Engagement? Always. Selling? Sometimes.** Jumping into social media with nothing to say but "Buy Now" is a recipe for failure. Engage-

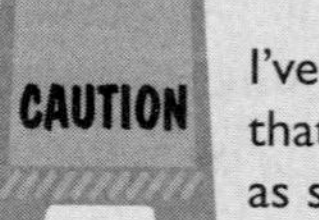

Don't Abandon Your Plan

I've seen some managers so susceptible to marketing trends that they abandon their plans to jump on the latest wave—such as social media. Don't do this. The holistic approach to marketing involves integrating social media into your overall marketing plan—without altogether abandoning traditional channels. Grow appropriately into social media efforts and test results as you go. Ensure that your promotions cross-reference one another so that they are complementary rather than competitive.

ment is imperative. Companies I've worked with have tried to move directly to transactions without taking appropriate steps to engage the audience beforehand. You ultimately want people to buy your pizza, cars, etc., but you have to build an effective strategy around the product to get to that sale.

5. **Resist Inflated Expectation Syndrome.** Are you populating your social media profiles or pages with products and expecting sales to take off like wildfire? It doesn't happen that way. Social media is a slow, steady race. Although exposure can be boosted by paid media, it's primarily an organic process that takes time. But the rewards, both in terms of engagement and ROI, can be powerful.

BUILD IT FOR THE LONG HAUL

SMART MANAGING

Take a long-term approach to your social media and you will be successful. Try to build a quick profile and then squeeze your new network for a quick sale and you will suffer. Consider your fans like a network of business contacts. You wouldn't expect someone you just met to give you a job referral; you'd need to build trust and a relationship first. Similarly, you can't expect your fans or followers to buy what you suggest until they are engaged with your company. The best way to foster engagement is to offer consistent value and authentic content—over time.

Achieving positive social media ROI is possible. Setting up your efforts for success by following simple guidelines can save you anguish and make the experience better for your social media community. And who knows? Your goals could be met more quickly than you expect.

Inviting Customers to Share Feedback

Two-thirds of respondents in a 2011 study by the Keller Fay Group reported thinking that positive word of mouth is credible, while less than half reported that they believe the negative feedback they hear. This is great news. But what's even more interesting is this: "Positive information was also more likely to be passed on to others, more than twice as likely to get people to look for more information, and had nearly four times the chance of pushing consumers to make a purchase."

Jackpot! Positive is powerful—even more powerful than a terrible experience or a negative review. So how do you help customers share those positive comments?

Give people a place to share positive comments. Provide customers with a place on your social media site(s) to share reviews and feedback, in addition to their own social networks and other online locations they're using, such as Yelp, Facebook, Twitter, and more. Add customer reviews to your e-commerce sites. Solicit feedback on your Facebook page or through your Twitter account to encourage customers to put their thoughts on "paper." For example, in the week before and after Christmas in the frenzy of buying, returning, and exchanging gifts, customer service experiences will join products as a topic of conversation. Having a place for customers to submit their testimonials publicly will help you.

Illustrate that you're open to receiving feedback on your social media sites. Women, for example, prefer to share positive experiences about products rather than negative ones, according to an October 2010 study by Harbinger via eMarketer. Demonstrating that as a company you welcome feedback shows you value customer feedback, which in itself carries weight with consumers. It also makes users feel more comfortable expressing their opinions. Begin doing this by tapping into the new customers who received your products as holiday gifts. Those who are still gushing over their gifts might take your advice and post their positive comments and feedback.

Encourage peer-to-peer sharing. This is another way to show confidence in your product and your enthusiasm for people talking about it with family and friends. Even recent national TV spots have done this. State Farm Insurance and Tempur-Pedic have included Ask Your Friends messaging on their social media sites. Adding social sharing buttons to your product pages and using other tools that make it easy for people to share product information and opinions, such as the Ask a Friend button in Shoutlet's Shop & Share feature, allows customers to effortlessly share their views with peers.

By being receptive to customer feedback about your products, you help generate online reviews and positive feedback. This, coupled with giving customers convenient tools for social sharing, can get those glowing reviews to more people online. And if they're positive, they're more likely to be influential.

QR Codes

Social media is booming. Mobile marketing is skyrocketing. Consumers are increasing their use of smartphones.

How can marketers act on these trends? Enter the QR code.

Marketers have adopted QR technology and integrated it into marketing campaigns, and the practice is growing. (Consumer awareness of QR codes continues to increase, too: 52 percent were aware of them as of fall 2010. Another study in February 2011 put awareness at two-thirds (about 65 percent of smartphone users).

> **HANDLING NEGATIVE REVIEWS**
>
> 
>
>
> Negative reviews can bring an upside in that they present media managers and brands the opportunity to engage and respond. This may or may not change the opinion of the complaining customer, but it can demonstrate your service and expertise to other customers.

> 
>
> **KEY TERM**
>
> **QR (Quick Response) code** 2-D barcodes that are scannable by most smartphones. They appear as square graphics with little squares inside them.

The functionality is simple for consumers. Walk up to a code, scan it, and view the ad. That's why marketers have used QR codes in dozens of new ways, each one with the intention of capitalizing on the seamless way they lead customers directly to your content.

QR codes can be used for a variety of purposes and in a variety of media. Consider these 27 examples of how to use them to your advantage.

Events Marketing

1. Host a scavenger hunt.

> **SCAVENGER HUNT**
>
> **FOR EXAMPLE**
>
> Neatorama and mental_floss hosted a Manhattan scavenger hunt for a chance to win a Ford Fiesta. Starbucks launched a two-week scavenger hunt to promote one of Lady Gaga's albums. The hunt, SRCH by Starbucks featuring Lady Gaga, started with a QR code on a Frappuccino banner. After scanning, users were directed to a website to uncover clues. (The My Starbucks iPhone app also includes a QR reader.)

2. Use event name tags. Use a template for all name tags used by guests who attend your special events, with QR codes linking to additional information about that attendee, or about the event.
3. Offer event swag such as souvenirs, T-shirts, hats, and other items guests can take away from the event. QR codes can be printed on these items.

Deals and Promotions

4. Offer discounts. When surveying smartphone users who have used QR codes, the number one reason they cited for scanning was to access coupons or discounts (trailed closely by accessing information).
5. Promote social media contests. This is an effective way to get people online interacting with your brand.
6. Share coupons and special offers. This might be a buy-one-get-one-free deal, for example.
7. Promote in-store sales and deals.

Print and Outdoor Advertising/Marketing

8. Print on billboards on pedestrian walkways to direct people to more information.
9. Print on real estate signs to link to details about a specific property.
10. Post on company vehicles.
11. Display on storefront windows.
12. Print in magazine ads (scan to buy).

On the Run Discounts

FOR EXAMPLE

Atlanta's Hartsfield-Jackson International Airport has included QR codes on signage to promote deals on concessions.

Marketing Materials

13. Provide directions to your business.
14. Print on business cards to give people access to information about you or your company.
15. Show videos related to printed materials—accessible through the QR code.

In-Store Engagement/Content Delivery

16. Link to product information.
17. Link to special "VIP" content.

HOME DEPOT

Home Depot displays QR codes for items on the shelves. The codes provide shoppers with helpful content about the product and relevant how-to information, such as videos, demos, and project guides. (QR codes on Home Depot advertising includes this info, plus a link to buy online.)

BACKSTAGE PASS

Macy's invited shoppers to learn more about top designers through its Macy's Backstage Pass QR code campaign. Shoppers could get video fashion advice, designers' thoughts, and more.

18. Include on restaurant menus to enable diners to access nutritional information or restaurant history.
19. Print QR codes on product packaging to provide detailed product information.
20. Print on point-of-sale receipts so purchasers can access surveys, product discounts, and more.

Education/Research

21. Enhance nonprofit applications, such as in museums where a QR code could link to a discussion about museum artifacts and share history based on applications that can identify locations.

BRINGING NEANDERTHALS INTO THE 21ST CENTURY

The Smithsonian Natural History Museum used QR codes as part of an exhibit on Neanderthals. The MEanderthals campaign's QR codes sent users to a site where they could upload a photo, see what they would have looked like 30,000 years ago, and share via Facebook and e-mail.

22. Offer community education/government outreach.

NYC

New York City is integrating codes into building permits, which give residents information about everything from restaurant health inspections to construction site details.

23. Provide links to customer feedback forms.
24. Enhance internal communications.

TV Teaser

To promote the new album of a music performer on TV's *Late Night with Jimmy Fallon*, Jimmy held up a QR code in lieu of an album cover. Within a day the clip of the segment had made it to YouTube Trends with 50,000 views.

TRICKS OF THE TRADE

Get to Know Your Colleagues

One clever way to enable employees to get to know one another is to add QR codes to nameplates to make it simple to learn more about colleagues.

Entertainment

25. Use on interactive TV.
26. Print on movie posters to link to information about plot, ratings, actors, and more.
27. Include on movie theater tickets to link to sponsors, trailers for other movies, concession offers, and more.

Creative applications of QR codes continue to emerge as marketers experiment with ways to unify their marketing initiatives and invest in content marketing that makes innovative use of delivery mechanisms.

Running Powerful Contests

The decision to launch a Facebook contest starts with a social media effort that can have a tremendous impact. Chances are you have a Facebook page that you've been using to connect with customers. You might need a way to engage them further. You might have a new product or want to highlight a product line in a unique way. Or you might be in the planning stages of your social media program for the next six months.

No matter why you're exploring the idea of a Facebook contest or sweepstakes, it's a marketing tactic that countless companies have leveraged with success. It's no surprise: The number of Facebook users has jumped 45 percent over the past 12 months. Facebook is now the most popular tool among marketers who use social media. Facebook contests and promotions can be beneficial to your company. With detailed planning and great execution, you can infuse your Facebook page with a fun campaign that generates fan interaction and creates long-term relationships with your customers via social media.

10 Ways to Get the Word Out. How you promote a Facebook contest makes all the difference in its success. But how can you promote it after it's gone live?

1. **Kick off the contest promotion by enlisting your current fans and e-mail marketing database.** Alert your active e-mail lists about the contest to encourage their participation and help you spread the initial word. Break the news of the contest to your existing fans to give them an exclusive sneak peek before launching through a Facebook wall post or status update.
2. **Promote with Facebook ads.** Target current likes who might not have had frequent interaction with your brand recently, as well as other Facebook users in your demographic.
3. **Cross-promote.** Don't limit your promotional efforts to the Facebook platform itself. Leverage your Twitter feed, YouTube channel, website, blog, and other places you communicate.
4. **Employ user-generated entries to promote the contest.** Pull selected photos or videos from your entries to promote the contest. For example, use a photo from last year's winner to promote this year's contest. You can even use entries from the current contest if appropriate. (Check with your legal representative about how to include language in the contest terms and conditions related to the use of this material.)
5. **Fan-gate your contest.** The idea behind this is that you offer exclusive content to those who like your business Facebook page. Make your contest tab your landing tab (pages within your fan page) and require a "like" to view the contest details. This allows new fans to see other contest-related posts, which they can share with others.
6. **Enlist e-commerce customers.** Add a link to the contest checkout pages (online order form) or order confirmation e-mails.
7. **Make it shareable.** Add social sharing options to your contest Facebook tab to make the process of spreading the word seamless.
8. **Think offline.** Brainstorm ways to use offline messaging, such as notes printed on store receipts at your brick-and-mortar locations. This is an example of using holistic marketing discussed earlier in this chapter.
9. **Add to your website.** Don't rely solely on Facebook icons on your web-

site to drive traffic to your Facebook page during the contest. Add messaging that promotes your contest on your website pages as well.

10. **Explore word-of-mouth and influencer outreach.** Unique contests and promotions can gain traction with bloggers and other industry influencers.

Mastering Blog Outreach

"Blogging activity presents new opportunities for marketers to influence—and monitor—conversations that may be relevant to their businesses," said Paul Verna, eMarketer senior analyst. "These conversations will continue to happen with or without participation from marketers, but those who join in—whether through their own sites or through a brand presence on independent ones—will have a place at the table." You may be wondering, what exactly is a blog?

> KEY TERM
>
> **Blog** A *blog* (a contraction of the term *weblog*) is a type of website usually maintained by an individual with regular entries of commentary, descriptions of events, or other material such as graphics or video. Entries are commonly displayed in reverse chronological order. *Blog* can also be used as a verb meaning "to maintain or add content to a blog."

Consider these common blog elements:

- A typical blog combines text, images, and links to other blogs, web pages, and other media related to its topic.
- Blogs offer readers an opportunity to leave comments. This is an important component of many blogs and one way to identify the influence level of a blogger (since a larger number of comments reflects more influence).
- Most blogs are primarily textual, although some blogs focus on art (artlog), photographs (photoblog), sketches (sketchblog), videos (vlog), music (MP3 blog), and audio (podcasting), all of which are part of a wider social media network.
- *Microblogging* on platforms such as Twitter is another type of blogging, one that consists of very short posts.

Use of Blogs. Regardless of your service or product, you can use a blog to:

- Launch a new product; educate the audience
- Reeducate your audience about product features and benefits
- Build brand awareness in the targeted social space—meaning the places where your target market is congregating online
- Tap into the influencers and work to penetrate their networks with meaningful content while building relationships
- Garner feedback and testimonials about your product or services

Blogging Best Practices. When creating a blog, take best practices into account. Check that:

- The blog content matches your product or brand's niche.
- Social media monitoring has uncovered bloggers or readers discussing your brand or a topic related to your brand.
- You create frequent posts (minimum of a couple of times a week).
- You aim for high unique monthly traffic.
- Visitors' length of stay on the site is substantial (the longer the better).
- The average number of comments per post is high (the higher the better).
- The types of sites the blog links to and size of blog roll is healthy (A *blog roll* is a listing of blogs that the blog author reads or recommends; usually listed to the side of the blog).
- The number of linkbacks to the site is strong (run the numbers at Technorati.com or Alexa.com).
- The types and frequency of outbound links included in the blog posts is substantial.
- The blog is not doing sponsored product reviews. The blogger should not be paid to post.
- The types of advertisers on the blog are appropriate for the blog's content and readership.

> TRICKS OF THE TRADE
>
> **UNIQUE VISITS**
>
> *Unique visits* on a website are those that come from different users as opposed counting the number of times a single user visits the blog.. This figure holds credibility in that it shows the number of times unique users come to your site—rather than the number of times the site is accessed.

DON'T PAY FOR REVIEWS

Paying a blogger to post a review of your product or service—or accepting money to publish such a review—crosses an ethical line. This would be similar to paying a newspaper publisher to run an article about your business in the Lifestyle section. Doing so would compromise editorial integrity. Editorial content should be published based on its news- or feature-worthy qualities. This ensures that the writer retains the ability to report honestly. Beware of blogs that offer you editorial exposure for a fee. Stay above the line and ensure that any reviews you receive or grant are legitimate and without monetary incentive.

Using Prizes and Rewards to Your Advantage

Reward your customers for interacting with your content by offering some special item for them giving you their time. Have you posted a new video or slideshow of an event or a new product line? Trigger more content to go live when your YouTube video hits a certain number of views or number of likes or your slideshow web app reaches a certain number of impressions (Shoutlet offers an app for this). Promote these hidden gems to your fans and friends to encourage sharing and viewing.

These are just a few ideas that could be modified for your brand.

Social Switchboard is a Shoutlet app designed to build unique, automated social campaigns while freeing up time for your team to engage with consumers in real time. Shoutlet's Social Switchboard allows your team to build entire sophisticated social media marketing campaigns in advance and set a vast array of prescheduled markers and milestones to trigger automatic changes to content across multiple social networks. You can let the behavior of your communities dictate when relevant and tailored content is published. Social Switchboard includes smart social media scheduling that distributes precreated content when your criteria is met—giving you more time to do the important business of building one-on-one relationships with your customers. Building campaigns in advance that automatically roll out over time frees you up to reply to individual user questions and comments as they come in.

Business to Business

B2B buyers are typically more complex than B2C. B2C buyers usually

FUNLEY'S DELICIOUS

FOR EXAMPLE

Funley's Delicious is an up-and-coming company with a knack for turning snack time into a cheerful moment in your day. But don't let the name fool you. This digital team means business, especially when it comes to maximizing its Facebook presence.

To promote the launch of several new products, Funley's initiated a strategy that not only boosted its Facebook page likes by 18,923 in 48 hours, but also helped them find their current customers, introduce products to new customers, and create an engaged Facebook community.

Initial Campaign: Free Sampling on Facebook

To support the rollout of new snack products and its new Facebook page, Funley's decided on two programs: a free sampling campaign and a weekly giveaway program. It kicked off the free sampling campaign first, which focused on three goals: (1) increase Facebook fans and collect data via a sign-up form for future marketing campaigns; (2) find an audience to sample Funley products to increase sales at retail; and (3) find brand ambassadors (a.k.a. Funley's Big Mouths) to promote the brand online and in their localities and stores where Funley's Delicious might not be currently sold.

Funley's offered a free sample and added a like-gated tab (only for those who have "liked" the page) using Shoutlet's contest platform to create a submission form to collect customer information. The response was incredible. Within 24 hours the Funley's Facebook page jumped from 288 "likes" to 17,663. After two days, fan totals reached 18,923. The response was so positive, Funley's was forced to turn off the sampling giveaway long before it had planned to. Even after 10,737 users signed up for the sample, over 8,000 more users liked the page over the next 24 hours.

The unexpected response was supported by the plan Funley's had put into place before it began the contest. The plan: launch a short-term free sample giveaway, but roll out a weekly prize giveaway indefinitely. Although the free sampling giveaway closed, 1,881 of its new likes entered the weekly prize giveaway. By having a plan in place, Funley's was able to engage with new fans even though the initial free sampling campaign had run its course.

know the type of product they want. They may want to learn about the different models or brands, but then they are ready to buy. B2B buyers typically have to buy more complicated products and services, and customer service will continue with a B2B buyer long after the purchase. Even leading up to the purchase is more complex because businesses generally buy in bulk or sign up for a contract, as opposed the B2C customer who pops into a store to purchase a product and pops out.

The value of social media as part of the B2B marketing mix includes branding, messaging, lead generation, and customer interaction. B2B companies with a strong social media presence vary the content of their updates, posts, and tweets among blog posts, external articles, employee spotlights, open-ended questions, and the occasional promotion. Content should target audience-oriented topics that lead to discussion and drive engagement. Engage your customers and prospects by answering questions and comments or by simply listening to them and acknowledging their feedback.

> TRICKS OF THE TRADE
>
> **TARGET YOUR CONTENT**
>
> If you're a B2B company, make sure you promote content that is informative and educational for your target audience. It is acceptable to mention what is happening in the news, but make sure you have a business spin to the article so your followers and friends constantly get valuable information from your posts.

Responding to Customers

You must ensure that you are always ready to respond to customers interacting through social media. Responding to every comment in many cases isn't realistic, but a consistent display of silence can damage customers' attitudes toward the brand. What happens when a brand does make an effort to respond? Customers love it.

- Six in 10 customers want brands to respond on Twitter. The same ratio said they'd be more likely to follow a brand that answered them, according to InboxQ. InboxQ delivers a real-time stream of questions related to your business, products, industry, or general interests from Twitter directly to your browser. You can download InboxQ from inboxq.com for Chrome and Firefox.
- More than 80 percent of those who complained on Twitter and received a response from the company said they "loved" or "liked" it, with 74 percent of them saying they were satisfied with the response.

If these studies are any indication, it could be argued that responding consistently means more sales, and unresponsiveness leads to lost sales. On a deeper level, not responding can lead to erosion of loyalty and disappointment by brand advocates and long-time customers. Those customers who might have become vocal cheerleaders for you in social media will turn away, causing your company to miss out on untold positive effects.

RESPONSE = COMMUNITY
Companies that make responding a priority develop strong relationships and grow their communities.

Focusing on Content

Another difference between B2B and B2C: B2B companies are seen as more professional. B2C buyers often make purchasing decisions based on emotion or whim, but B2B purchases are usually more calculated.

ADHERE TO THE B2B CULTURE
B2C companies can often get away with putting up pictures of employees, asking questions via social media, and using emotion such as jokes or stories to pull in readers. B2B companies, on the other hand, need to target their content.

Every aspect of B2B social media should be thought out and focused on logistics—that is, how to make the campaign measurable. Use statistics, facts, research findings, etc., to let readers know why something is important. Many B2B companies also create a series of posts to bring buyers back to the social media account to learn more.

Building Relationships

B2C companies are typically thought of as having an audience that is more involved in social media. However, this can often make it difficult for a B2C company because there is so much competition. You must find a way to make yourself stand out in the B2C world, but you undoubtedly have an interested audience. B2B companies usually find that other companies active on social media are trying to grab customers, not necessarily strike up a relationship with another company—unless this company helps meet their strategic objectives. B2B marketers often mine competitors' sites to find information about potential customers—viewing their client lists, for example, to get ideas on which businesses to contact.

When leveraging social media for a B2B, focus on finding start-up or other companies in your area. While B2C can gain followers and friends by promoting deals and getting others to spread the word, it's more difficult for B2B. It's a long process to recruit loyal followers who will convert to your brand, but when this occurs it will be a bigger deal than if you were working with B2C because generally B2B exchanges go after larger customers who either need more of a product or service or need it for a longer time. Also, in B2B there are usually several people in the company who can become loyal customers and even evangelize for your company.

Nonprofits

There are many ways a nonprofit can use social media to increase income and mission awareness, including:

- **Finding grants**
- **Conducting high-income/target customer individual outreach**
- **Public fundraising**

TRICKS OF THE TRADE

The LinkedIn Advantage

The high-income demographic is undoubtedly on LinkedIn, and LinkedIn's advanced people search gives you an opportunity to pinpoint people in a way that Facebook can't. LinkedIn is particularly useful for those working in nonprofits and seeking grant funding or greater support.

Promoting Events

Use social media to effectively promote events in a number of ways. The most important thing is to register your event across all platforms where your target demographic might be.

- **Subscriber retention**
- **Event promotion**
- **General public outreach.** This is the one part of a social media strategy where I see a need for nonprofits to blog and tell their stories. This can even be done on YouTube. However it's done, social media gives nonprofits a way to get found on the Internet where people spend 25 percent of online time in social media, Google, and the other search engines, including the second largest of them all, YouTube. Plus, this builds more content that you can share in your other social media channels.

- **Collaboration with other nonprofits.** I consider this similar to strategic alliances in a business sense. Like finding grant funding opportunities, this is another B2B aspect for which nonprofits can use not only LinkedIn but also Twitter due to the ease of communicating with others who are active on these social media platforms. Reach out to other nonprofits that may be aligned with your cause in another part of the country or world and see what you can learn from each other or potentially collaborate on.
- **Advertising**

Using Social Media to Decrease Expenses

Social media can be a valuable way to decrease expenses in other areas. Social media can help you with:

- **Finding interns and volunteers.** While this may be a short-term approach, it can give your organization a huge boost by using the skills and experience of a potential mentor or the passion of a young student or apprentice. Where should you reach out? LinkedIn, of course! For finding younger interns and volunteers, Facebook is your prime choice. Either way, don't forget about Twitter! And remember: These "temporary" professional volunteers may turn into great employees, board members, or subscribers! Foster engagement with them as you would anyone who brushes up against your organization.
- **Social recruiting.** Conventional recruiting is costly. Why not use social media to reach out directly to your target future employees?

Other Tactics for Making the Most of Social Media

Here are a few other tips for using social media effectively:

- Choose appropriate social media goals and connect them to organizational goals.

Aligning Social Media Goals to Organizational Goals

SMART

MANAGING

Earlier in the book, we talked about being clear about your goals. Having thousands of fans is nice, but isn't useful unless it helps you meet your objectives. Consistently revisit your organizational vision to ensure that your social media plans align with your vision.

- Define and understand your community.
- Determine what to measure.
- Allocate resources to get the job done.
- Experiment, monitor, and modify.

Cultivating Brand Advocates

Social sharing is the heartbeat of social media. For large brands, it becomes especially powerful when it's done by a loyal customer who is passionate enough about a product or company to spread the word to his or her networks, both online and offline. These brand advocates (another name for evangelists) are like gold.

SMART

MANAGING

Be Flexible

Boldness to try new things in marketing is a valuable trait, but it should be tempered with the willingness to step back and reevaluate results—adjusting appropriately to what what does and doesn't work. Be firm in implementing campaigns and online tools, but flexible in how you respond to feedback and analytics.

How can companies maximize the potential for more customers to rise to advocates? Here are a few tips.

Don't confuse a fan/follower with an influencer or an advocate. Fans and followers fall into several categories, from true brand advocates to those who aren't very engaged with your social media communities. They aren't necessarily influencers and/or advocates. The distinction between influencers and advocates is less clear. Influencers are those who have clout (possibly high Klout as well).

SMART

MANAGING

Create Advocates Who Love You

Michael Brito, vice president for social media at Edelman Digital (the interactive arm of a large, independently owned public relations firm), points out that while influencers are great at driving traffic, they don't love your brand like an advocate. Advocates are passionate customers who "love you even if you don't give them the time of day," he writes. It's these diehard, vocal advocates of whom every brand marketer dreams, and only a fraction of your fans and followers might fall into this category.

What you do in social media cultivates brand advocates. The reason customers grow into advocates varies from person to person, but your company's social media activities have a huge impact on relationships—current and up-and-coming—that advocates have with your brand. Sharing engaging content that adds value and displaying sincerity in each interaction strengthen the relationship with your best advocates and fuel the fire of their support.

You don't have to be a sexy brand to have brand advocates. Every company can have an army of brand advocates, no matter what the industry or target audience. In one case study by Zuberance, a research company, an auto windshield repair service identified 76 percent of its customer base as advocates, and a motel chain pinpointed 62 percent as advocates. While it might seem easier for a hot apparel brand to have brand advocates touting it, great companies and products of any kind are as likely to have dedicated customers who praise your services unprompted.

The value of brand advocates to a company is tough to estimate. After all, how can you put a value on an authentic belief in a company or product? Nurturing relationships with your customers in social media can only help your company create more bona fide advocates.

Manager's Checklist for Chapter 9

- ☑ Determine your ROI calculation before you begin.
- ☑ Run contests and offer coupons to quickly build a direct marketing database.
- ☑ Illustrate that you're open to feedback on social media sites.
- ☑ Use QR codes to drive foot traffic to retail locations from printed materials.
- ☑ Nonprofits can decrease expenses by using social media as a communication channel for recruiting interns, volunteers, and donors.
- ☑ Never confuse a fan or follower with a true advocate.

Establishing Brand Control

You cannot always control what goes on outside. But you can always control what goes on inside.

—Wayne Dyer, teacher and author

If you work in a highly regulated industry such as banking or insurance, you realize how important it is to maintain control of your brand and influence the people who may interact with social media outside of your company. There have been several social media disasters that, with better planning, could have been avoided. The trick with managing social media's external reach is to have a good policy and platform to govern your communication programs.

Using a platform, you can set up a system that gives you multiple checks and balances to approve content before it goes live on the social media sites. Likewise, having an internal social media policy ensures your employees know the rules of engagement when communicating on Facebook, Twitter, YouTube, etc. It takes both—a policy and a platform—to protect your company from a potential public relations disaster.

Using a social media marketing platform instead of allowing direct access to the company's Twitter account could have avoided a social media fiasco at Chrysler (see sidebar). Social media marketing platforms give companies the ability to create multiple points of approval before messages are released to the public. Given the Chrysler situation, it would

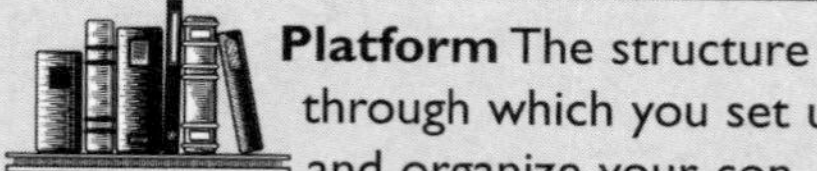

KEY TERM

Platform The structure through which you set up and organize your content—in this case, social media. In this chapter, we discuss social media platforms that allow you to set up content prior to launching it live.

have been easy to block the post if only another person had looked at it first. It's better to have a platform that can provide restriction levels than to post directly. However, even with tools like a platform and multiple levels of approval, a social media policy is still important. For example, employees could still ruin a company's reputation from their personal accounts. Even with the best platform in place, you'll never be able to control what your employees do outside the office.

FOR EXAMPLE

Case Study: Social Media Disaster

In 2011, a public relations employee working with Chrysler Motors put a post on Twitter that embarrassed the entire Chrysler company. The tweet read, "I find it ironic that Detroit is known as the #motorcity and yet no one here knows how to fucking drive." This message went out under the company's Twitter account to thousands of followers and rapidly became headline news. Chrysler quickly removed the tweet, apologizing that its account had been compromised.

FOR EXAMPLE

Multi-Account Panel: Legal Compliance

Shoutlet, Inc. is a platform that can manage multiple brands via separate account-level tracking, approvals, and reports. An administrator can access each subaccount. Content libraries can store preapproved videos, images, and status updates for sub-account holders to ensure compliance.

Who Should Create Your Social Media Policy?

An effective social media policy is created by a team!

Gather input from several people in your company as you write your social media communication policy. Figure 10-1 shows the different positions that should be included as you write your policies.

You'll need quite a bit of input to develop your social media communication policy.

> **CREATING A SOCIAL MEDIA POLICY**
> Every company has its own standards when it comes to creating a social media policy. Make sure you evaluate your internal needs as well as your external (after hours) social media rules before creating a formal policy. What rules or guidelines do you need to put in place to ensure your social media communications are professional and productive? You can access templates for creating a social media policy at the Database of Corporate Social Media Policies: socialmediagovernance.com/policies.php.

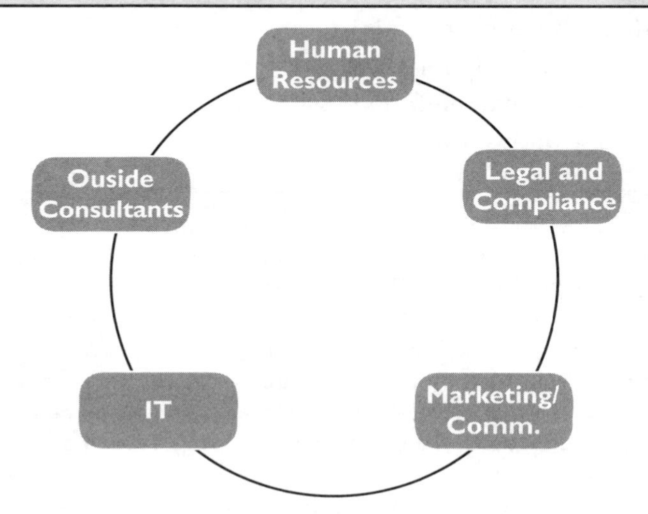

Figure 10-1. Social media policy team

Legal Issues and Site Policies

There are known legal "trouble areas" when using social media. You must closely consider the following areas as you create your own social media communication policy:

- Intellectual property protection or misuse and infringement
- Liability for HR claims (discrimination, harassment, privacy)
- Liability for false advertising/disparagement claims
- Reputation management issues

Most companies only consider the public relations risk without thinking about human resource violations, sexual harassment issues, and intellectual property challenges. Therefore, I highly recommend obtaining a formal legal opinion before beginning your social media policy planning.

Advertising Regulations and Reputation Management

The same advertising and intellectual property rules that apply to traditional advertising (e.g., print, television, radio) apply to social media. There are new aspects that specifically concern issues with Internet marketing. In addition, there are unresolved legal concepts as applied to social media. It is critical to understand the legal considerations and to undertake only acceptable risks.

Make sure you have confirmed legal use rights to any logos, videos, or text that you use in your campaigns.

FOR EXAMPLE

eBay Copyright

About six years ago, I worked on a campaign for eBay's Half.com company. They contracted with my firm to distribute videos of a comedy piece they did for the back-to-school book-buying season. Once the campaign was completed, they asked me to pull down the videos from the entire Internet. Clearly, this was an impossible feat to accomplish because the videos had already been shared with thousands of people through YouTube and blogs. I found out later that they had to pay royalties to the actors in the video. Since this promotion came before the Screen Actors Guild laws had changed, eBay was worried about the extra expenses in the form of royalties that were accruing automatically every time the video was played.

External Social Network Policies and Restrictions

Most people who begin a campaign or promotion on a social network fail to understand that they must observe the network's site policies in addition to other legal considerations. When planning a campaign, not only must you worry about copyright laws and potential public relations issues, but you also must consider rules for each social network so they don't kick you off for breaking their rules. There are several activities that you may accidentally do to get banned from Facebook, Twitter, or Google. Make sure you read each social media platform's policies before going live with your campaign.

Social Network Policies

Listed below are links to the Terms of Services for the policies of the most popular social media destinations.

- Facebook (facebook.com/legal/terms)
- Twitter (twitter.com/tos)
- YouTube (youtube.com/static?gl=US&template=terms)
- Pinterest (pinterest.com/about/terms)
- Google (google.com/intl/en/policies/terms)
- Yahoo! (info.yahoo.com/legal/us/yahoo/utos/utos-173.html)

Facebook Actions That Could Get You Banned. Before engaging in a Facebook campaign, read and understand these rules:

- **You must use your real name and date of birth.** It's common for people to create "handles" on social networks like Twitter or for a Gmail address, but you cannot create a fake persona on Facebook. Additionally, if you use a portion of a fake name, like "Jason Beta" or "Test Jason," this could result your permanent ban from Facebook.
- **Make sure your "friends" are human.** No companies, businesses, or organizations can be your "friends." You (the individual with a profile) can like fan pages (companies' pages), but companies should never "friend" your profile. You as an individual "follow" a company's fan page. You can create Groups that will let you have a place to share information among specific people.
- **Don't create too many profile accounts.** People I work with create two accounts: one for work relationships, one for personal. I don't see a problem with two. However, I have seen brand managers and software developers create several pages under one name to test products or development. Creating multiple accounts—even for testing purposes—can get you kicked off Facebook forever for breaking copyright laws. Don't do it.
- **Don't post material copyrighted by others.** Attaching videos, photos, or music to content you do not own onto any social media can get you in trouble. Granted, it's easy to do now with YouTube already violating copyrighted content, but even YouTube reserves the right to ban you from its network for doing so. The sad truth is that many

Take Precautions When Using Google Images

Google Images offers countless photos and illustrations for use. Some of these images are available for personal use or promotional materials; however, many of these images are copyrighted. The advanced features of Google Image Search include the ability to filter by usage rights. Be sure you understand the various copyrights associated with these images and always give credit to the copyright holder unless you obtain a license that specifies otherwise.

people ignore the warning or simply don't know anything about copyright law.

Google Actions That Could Get You Banned. The following items explain the actions that could get you kicked off Google:

- Like being an accomplice to a crime, just linking to an illegal site or a site that has violated Google's terms of service can get you banned. Make sure you know which sites you are linking to from your own website and often check the links to make sure the site hasn't changed.

No Faking

You cannot intentionally create company websites to raise a page rank. Creating fake pages and interlinking them to improve page rank is a violation of Google's terms of service. Nor can you link to pages that others have created illegally.

MISTAKE PROOFING

Hire Ethical and Responsible Programmers

If you hire a web programmer, make sure he or she follows legal and ethical practices. My experience is that most people who work in this space want to do the right thing. Make sure your programmers are educated on the latest policies.

- **Mini-nets, or fishing lures,** is a process of interlinking multiple domains with a single ownership to artificially raise the PageRank of each interlinked page. Similarly, you can set up numerous domain names and stuff them with keywords to achieve a higher PageRank. Both are a violation of Google's terms of service and could get you banned.

- **Virtual IP addresses** are a red flag to Google and could get you banned. Setting up virtual IP addresses is the process of placing and registering several IP addresses with Google that link back to one domain. (This is different from domain masking, mentioned in an earlier chapter, which keeps one IP address but covers up the domain name with a label.) Google could see virtual IP addresses as a violation, so it's best to avoid this practice. If you are running several campaigns at once and want to track back to a single URL, use a domain shortener (Bit.ly or TinyURL). This is different from creating virtual IP addresses because a domain shortener still uses your IP address—but just provides you with a shortened URL you can use for marketing purposes.
- **Don't duplicate content.** Google wants fresh content that changes often to appear in its search return. Be diligent about providing fresh content so you are not penalized for reuse.

Creating a Short URL. URL shortening is a web technique by which a uniform resource locator (URL) may be made substantially shorter and still direct a user to the required page. This is achieved by using an HTTP redirect on a domain name that is short, which links to the web page that has a long URL. This is especially convenient for messaging technologies such as Twitter and Identi.ca that limit the number of characters that can be used in a message. Short URLs allow otherwise long web addresses to be referred to in a tweet.

URL Shorteners

TOOLS

Here are some tools for creating URL shorteners:

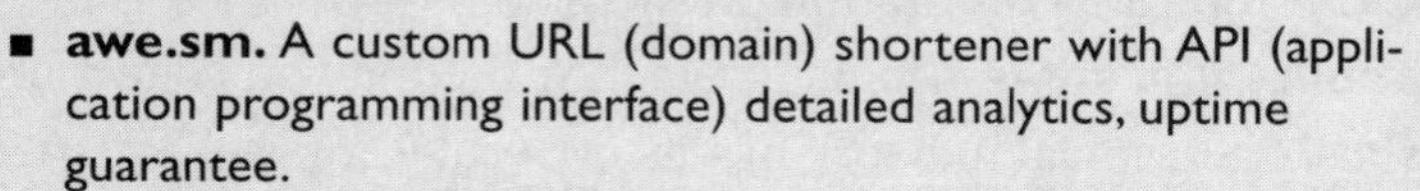

- **awe.sm.** A custom URL (domain) shortener with API (application programming interface) detailed analytics, uptime guarantee.
- **budURL.com.** The budURL Enterprise edition offers the opportunity to use your own domain. Their *dashboard*—the page through which you view your information—provides extensive analytics and real-time stats.
- **Google Short Links.** Google runs a URL shortener as part of Google Apps For Your Domain. It's a feature you can be add to your dashboard widget (where you track your analytics).
- **Bitly.** Offers URL redirection service with real-time link tracking.
- **Tiny URL.** Changes a big URL into tiny URL. It comes with link editing and detailed click statistics.

Other Risks

Make sure you understand the rules for all advertising you do. Also make sure you choose advertising vendors that abide by these rules. Expanding on these points when dealing with external social networks and online advertising, consider the following aspects before launching your campaigns:

- **General terms of use.** Many sites have ground rules for using their networks. For example, YouTube requires certain file formats to support your videos. YouTube prohibits pornography from its network.
- **Intellectual property policy.** This is similar to copyrighted material. Never post content you do not own, especially if you are posting on behalf of a company. Even if you post photos of employees online, get a signed Model Release Form from each employee in a photo (get a sample release form from iStockphoto.com, www.istockphoto.com/docs/languages/english/modelrelease.pdf). I've seen disgruntled employees sue a company that posted their picture on a company website for an advertising campaign.
- **Advertising policy.** There are several laws to observe when it comes to advertising. You may not market alcohol or tobacco products to minors. Additionally, there are laws to consider when marketing to children (read about COPA at en.wikipedia.org/wiki/Child_Online_Protection_Act).
- **Promotions policy.** Social networks like Facebook have rules for running contests and promotions. Make sure you understand each site's rules before you run a promotion on them.
- **Privacy policy.** You are restricted in the information you collect from social sites. Each social network has its own rules for the way member information can be used.
- **Developer policy.** Make sure you understand any policy about altering computer code if you intend to modify a site or embed your own code into that code, such as Javascript, iFrame, HTML, etc. Many codes have strict rules when it comes to how their networks accept third-party code.

Do you currently comply with these terms? Many companies ignore these requirements to their peril. It's time to start reading the fine print!

Promoting and Administering a Facebook Contest

One social media effort that can deliver tremendous impact is a Facebook contest. You probably have a company Facebook page you've been using to connect and interact directly with customers. Now you're looking for a way to further engage those customers.

While the payoff can be big, holding a successful contest takes in-depth planning. Once you outline the details of your contest, it's time to look closely at the fine print. Contest terms and conditions are a vital and required part of running a contest. There are two sets of requirements: standard legal requirements and Facebook's own promotional guidelines. You must follow both sets of guidelines when running a Facebook contest.

The Legal Rules. The legalese surrounding a contest covers a variety of topics and must include certain rules. Your terms and conditions might be required to include:

- Entry regulations based on a participant's state or country of residence
- Selection of winners and how winners are to be notified
- Restrictions on how certain groups can participate (e.g., age requirements)
- How entries can be used by the company in the future
- Alternative modes of entry

Facebook Rules. Facebook has specific rules that govern contest administration on its platform. At this writing, the most recent changes to this policy were released in May 2011, but they can change at a moment's notice. Refer to the guidelines (www.facebook.com/promotions_guidelines.php) when planning and again just before launching your contest. You must also abide by Facebook's Statement of Rights and Responsibilities, the Ad Guidelines, the Platform Policies, and all other applicable Facebook policies. See:

- Facebook.com/legal/terms
- Facebook.com/ad_guidelines.php
- Developers.facebook.com/policy

The primary theme of Facebook's promotion rules is that most of

Facebook's platform functionality cannot be used to administer a promotion (more on this shortly).

FACEBOOK IS YOUR FRIEND, BUT NOT YOUR PARTNER

Facebook, as a company, cannot be perceived as a partner that condones your promotion in any way. Facebook offers the platform for you to promote, but be careful about suggesting to your audience that Facebook has any part in backing your product or service.

Facebook's Promotion Rules: A Breakdown. Contests on Facebook must be run through a third-party application. You must run your promotion through apps on Facebook.com, either on a canvas page or an app on a page tab.

KEY TERM

Tabs These are where brands on Facebook are free to create experiences for their fans and customers. From contests and giveaways to exclusive content, page tabs have many purposes.

These third-party applications can be apps your company has custom developed for the contest or apps provided by third-party vendors, such as Shoutlet.

SHOUTLET'S SOCIAL CANVAS

Shoutlet's Social Canvas puts professional-level design tools in your hands. Your team can create custom Facebook apps, HTML5 pages, and web apps with no coding required. Social Canvas is the only tool in the industry that enables you to build rich, interactive social media content and publish it to an unprecedented number of social accounts, social networks, and websites.

- You cannot use Facebook features and functionality as part of the contest mechanism: Asking participants to use Facebook functionality to enter your contest is prohibited. For instance, users cannot automatically be entered into a contest by checking into a Facebook place, posting a photo directly to Facebook, commenting on a post, tagging a brand's page or photo, or using other Facebook features.
- Other than three activities—"liking" a page, connecting to an app, or checking into a place via a Facebook location app—Facebook fea-

DON'T RISK IGNORING POLICIES

I recently read about a popular real estate page with tens of thousands of followers. Its administrator inadvertently engaged in a trademark infringement. Despite complying once he knew of his violation, Facebook shut down the page. He started a new page, but this problem would have been best avoided.

Similarly, Scandinavian Airlines had a promotion shut down by Facebook for using native features (comments, posts, photos) within a video it produced (simplyzesty.com/facebook/how-to-run-a-brilliant-but-illegal-facebook-competition-case-study/#). This violated Facebook's terms.

Facebook states in its policies: "In addition to our other remedies, we may remove any materials relating to the promotion or disable your page, application or account if we determine in our sole discretion that you violate any of our policies." The moral of these stories is: Know your policies before you promote.

tures cannot be used as a condition of entry. For instance, requiring users to add their e-mail to an app or comment on a wall post is prohibited.

- There are several rules on contest management. Two of them are: (1) You can't use the Facebook Like button as a way to collect votes on entries. (2) You can't notify winners on Facebook, such as through a wall post, message, or in chat.
- You must make it clear that Facebook does not condone your contest and that it is not liable for any claims related to the contest.

Promotions on Facebook must include the following:

- A complete release of Facebook by each entrant or participant from all liability or claims. To accomplish this, have your legal counsel create a terms and conditions list that is approved via checkbox by each participant to release Facebook from liability.
- Acknowledgment that the promotion is in no way sponsored, endorsed, administered by, or associated with Facebook.
- Disclosure that the participant is providing information to you and the data will not be shared with Facebook. This disclosure is the only place you can mention Facebook.

You might ask, "But I've seen other brands do this. Why can't I?" Although many of these rules have been in place, Facebook page administrators have bent the rules. Breaking the rules is not worth the risk. If Facebook is an important enough social network for your company to consider investing in, ensure you don't do anything to jeopardize the resources you've already dedicated to connecting with customers in this space.

User-Generated Content

An increasingly popular way to engage customers and to effectively brand your products is by using user-generated content. The questions become, though: Do you have an appropriate policy in place? Who owns the content? What are the risks? Are you protected by the Communications Decency Act?

Publicity Rights

Publicity or promotion rights are state law–driven. Social media sites also have policies on imposter accounts to prevent this activity from taking place. You cannot use another's image or likeness for commercial purposes without permission. Legal remedies for the complainant can include injunctive relief, monetary damages, and attorney fees, so be careful. Potential hot spots include shared videos, pictures, and your social media accounts.

FTC and False Advertising

The Federal Trade Commission (FTC) has broad authority to prevent and punish unfair and deceptive commercial practices. Product claims against false advertising, for example, cannot be merely "aspirational" and, therefore, must reflect "generally expected performance." You must be able to substantiate your claim with, for example, market studies or scientific data. For example, if you run a diet site, it's unacceptable to state "Results are not typical." Product endorsers must provide their honest, accurate opinion. The company must disclose if the author/endorser is receiving money or other consideration in return for the endorsement. This can be tough in social media forums where there are character limitations (like Twitter's 140 characters). If you publish testimonials or link to them, there is a second level of proof required—meaning the customer has to agree to have the testimonial published. These rules apply to bloggers and other affiliates.

Companies must understand that "material connections" (sometimes payments or free products) between advertisers and endorsers or other connections that consumers would not expect must be disclosed. These examples address what constitutes an endorsement when bloggers or other "word-of-mouth" marketers convey the message. A blog poster who receives cash or in-kind payment to review a product is considered as having given an endorsement. Thus, bloggers who make an endorsement must disclose the material connection they share with the seller of the product or service.

FTC Rules on Blogging

CAUTION

Several new FTC rules exist on what is permissible in promotions—including through blogs. For example, while it used to be acceptable for promoters to highlight atypical customer experiences as long as they included a disclaimer to that effect, the promoters are now required to explicitly explain the typical experiences a customer might expect. In addition, bloggers must disclose any material connection (such as a free product) they have to a company whose product or service they endorse. Finally, based on the new laws, endorsers can be held liable for claims they make in promotions. It is important to keep abreast of the latest laws governing promotions. Read more about these changes at ftc.gov/opa/2009/10/endortest.shtm.

FTC violations can bring a lawsuit if you fail to comply with an order. You will be forced to pay a penalty of $16,000 (per violation of an order, not per Tweet or blog entry). FTC authority also extends to consumer redress, on which there is no monetary cap. Internationally, the UK Advertising Association has agreed to apply the Advertising Standards Authority (the UK's independent regulator of advertising across all media, now including marketing on websites—see ASA.org.uk) to social media and has its own recommended standards.

Copyrights

Copyright protects almost any human expression with some spark of creativity that has been written down, drawn, affixed, or otherwise recorded. Unauthorized reproduction, distribution, display, performance, and creation of derivative works can violate a copyright.

Ensure the works you put out there are your own works or works for which you have obtained a license in the same way you would in print

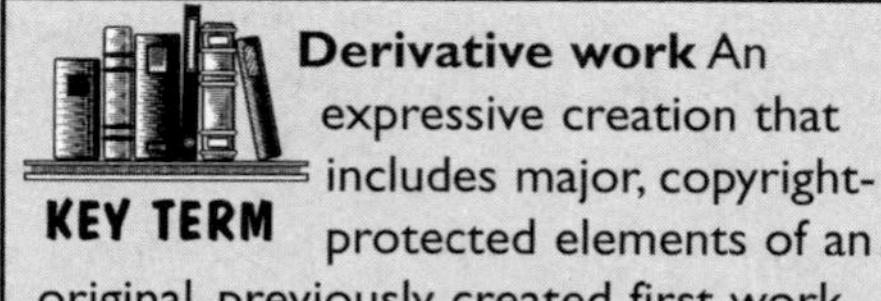

Derivative work An expressive creation that includes major, copyright-protected elements of an original, previously created first work (the underlying work).

advertising. Make sure you understand the license terms as well.

Other Potential Issues

When considering legal implications of online marketing, you must also acquire a basic understanding of the following potential problem areas:

- Collection and use of consumer data (privacy)
- Defamation
- Harassment
- Fraud
- Disclosure of confidential information or other protected information

Regulating External Communication

Once a strategic plan is in place, initiate policies to regulate your external communications including: employees using social media on behalf of the company, employees making personal use of social media, outside sales representatives, bloggers, endorsers. Make sure to:

- Give anyone directly contributing to your social media clear rules on what they can and can't post.
- Implement written agreements with bloggers, endorsers, and outside sales representatives.
- Retain rights to police content and remove anything objectionable.

Best Practices: Creating an Online Marketing Policy

It's important to give employees clear rules. To create the right plan for your company, first determine what your company will and will not allow in its online marketing practices. Realize that there is no one-size-fits-all online marketing policy.

In your policy, be careful to balance risks and rewards. Provide too much restriction on what you allow, and employees will retaliate; provide too little restriction, and you could open yourself up for disaster. Consider the following questions when writing your policy:

- What social media platforms will be used and who will control them?
- Will competitor trademarks be used and to what extent?
- Will you have endorsers?
- Who will monitor what others are saying about you?
- Will you solicit user-generated content? If so, how will you monitor it?
- What information will you collect and how will it be used?

Once you've collected this data, you can outline a social media policy.

Agreements and Policies

Your policy should govern employees using social media on behalf of the company, employees making personal use of social media, and how you will handle input from outside sales representatives, bloggers, and endorsers. For example, ensure your employees have a clear set of rules. Follow up and implement written agreements with bloggers, endorsers, and outside sales representatives. Lastly, retain your right to police content and remove anything objectionable. Consider the following four items when developing a policy:

> **TRICKS OF THE TRADE**
>
> **CREATING A SOCIAL MEDIA POLICY**
>
> A social media policy should integrate with your other company policies and include:
>
> - Confidentiality and nondisclosure
> - General e-mail and Internet use
> - Employee privacy
>
> Remember: When it comes to policy, repetition is good!

1. Prevention is cheaper and more effective than reaction.
2. Create a culture where everyone understands why social media is in place and how these policies are important to the company.
3. Document all policies in writing.
4. Act promptly and consistently when employees fail to observe a policy or a third party uses social media unlawfully.

Employment Law Compliance

In addition to developing a social media policy, be sure you understand federal and state employment laws. Establish policies in advance to deal with potential trouble areas (e.g., sexual harassment). Distribute the policies to all who need to know, particularly management, marketing, SEO companies, web developers, and employees.

DESIGNATE "POSTERS" FOR THE COMPANY

Social media is ultimately a viral, immediate, PR outlet for your company. Require that official postings of company news, etc., on social media be posted by a designated company representative. Create a decision tree for responding to content questions and comments about company material appearing on social media platforms.

Monitoring Your Brand

Managing your social networks requires continued promotion of and response to Facebook comments and other activity on your Facebook wall or other social platforms, such as Twitter. For example, safeguarding your contest from inappropriate content or abuse of the voting process can prevent issues during a contest promotion. By using a platform like Shoutlet, your company can review content before publishing.

Why Monitor Your Brand on Social Networks?

Monitoring your brand involves continuously discovering conversations related to your brand with the purpose of engaging and supporting not only your brand, but also your customers. Typically, this is done in real time to provide an immediate response to particular topics or situations.

Many of these conversations via social media may be about your brand or your product, some might be about a similar brand or a product similar to yours—superior or inferior doesn't really matter. What matters is the fact that others are talking about this without you being part of these conversations except to answer questions. To learn more, provide a

MAKING YOUR FACEBOOK CONTESTS FAIR

Some third-party applications that companies use to run contests on Facebook have built-in functionality to review user-generated content before it's submitted for public viewing. You can acquire third-party applications with features that restrict, say, too many votes from one user to ensure voting isn't deliberately skewed. The two-way conversations that can happen in social media between brands and consumers generate trust, brand loyalty, and ultimately, increased sales. This kind of social media relationship-building happens every day without contests or sweepstakes. But promotions can kick-start this valuable interaction with your brand.

better service, help customers, build loyalty, and prevent problems, it is essential to monitor what people say about your brand or your products.

How to Monitor Your Brand on Social Networks

An important part of monitoring your brand or destination on social networks is to find a structure that works. This means that you will want to choose the social media channel that works best for your brand. Here are a few pointers to help you monitor your brand:

- Focus on key topics related to your brand, and monitor those topics. These topics need to tie in with what your brand is about and what your product is used for. For example, if you offer an irritable bowel syndrome (IBS) treatment, your topics might include "digestion remedies," "intestinal problems," or "IBS" in general.
- Find out what people are already talking about. This is a question that many brands fail to ask. Research what your customers are discussing—including what is and isn't working for them in the products or services they are using—and you will have a big clue into how to address their needs.
- Establish beforehand what is unpleasant about your brand/product. Who is already saying something and why?
- Establish what is good about your brand/product. What can you build on?
- Understand the metrics you're tracking and how to use the tools.
- Analyze your data and respond based on what you learn.

Some Good Free Tools to Help You Monitor Your Brand

Google Alerts. This Google tool works well for monitoring your keywords and sending you an alert whenever they get used online. You configure Google Alerts by entering the keywords or phrases you want to monitor, select the format of results you want (news, blogs, video discussions, print, or digital books), and the frequency you want alerts sent to you via e-mail or RSS.

Social Mention. Like Google Alerts, Social Mention lets you set up alerts for keywords and phrases and be notified when they are used. Social Mention goes beyond Google Alerts and analyzes the following list, while providing a point-in-time social media search and analysis service, daily social media alerts, and a third-party API:

- **Strength of the keyword.** Strength is the likelihood that your brand is being discussed in social media. A simple calculation is used: phrase mentions within the last 24 hours divided by total possible mentions.
- **Sentiment of the keyword.** Sentiment is the ratio of mentions that are generally positive to those that are generally negative.
- **Passion.** Passion is a measure of the likelihood that individuals talking about your brand will do so repeatedly. For example, if you have a small group of passionate advocates who talk about your products or brand all the time, you will have a higher passion score. Conversely, if every mention is written by a different author, you will have a lower score.
- **Reach.** Reach is a measure of the range of influence. It is the number of unique authors referencing your brand divided by the total number of mentions.
- **Average number of days between mentions**
- **Top keywords**
- **Top users**
- **Top hashtags** (the symbol # used to mark keywords or topics in a tweet—originally created by Twitter users as a way to categorize messages)

Twilert. Twilert is a free, web-based app that sends you e-mail updates as often as you want when the keywords you choose are mentioned or discussed on Twitter.

Social Media Monitoring Must-Dos

Here are some tricks to help you stay current and aware at all times:

- Download the apps for all the social media monitoring tools you use, and set them up to notify you on each of your mobile or electronic devices.
- Download an RSS reader (via a free app, such as Mobilerssapp.com) to your mobile device to keep up with updates to your topic or brand.
- Make it easy to stay connected at all times and use the wonders of today's technology to your advantage. Then you can be reasonably assured that if something goes on in the online world, you will be one of the first to hear about it!

Tweetdeck. Tweetdeck is a desktop application that lets you monitor multiple Twitter accounts, hashtags, or keywords at a time.

HootSuite. HootSuite combines a number of monitoring tools into one across multiple social media platforms and multiple accounts.

Get Notified in Real Time

All these tools, used together or alone, will do a good job helping you monitor your brand. But the real value happens when you do the monitoring in real time—meaning you get notifications quickly about the results of your social media, and you analyze and act on them. No tool can help if you are late to react. And in many cases when a social media crisis happens, it happens across multiple platforms. Your ability to react and respond before it gets out of control should be your goal.

More Tools to Check Out

Here are several free tools to help you with your social media monitoring:

- Netvibes
- PostRank Analytics
- Social Oomph
- TweetStats
- WildFire
- Klout
- Pinerly

The following are paid tools:

- Shoutlet
- Alterian
- Needium
- Radian6

Manager's Checklist for Chapter 10

- ☑ It is critical to understand all the legalities when using social media channels and to undertake only acceptable risks.
- ☑ The primary theme of the Facebook promotions rules is that most of Facebook's platform functionality cannot be used to administer a promotion.

- ☑ A contest's legalese includes a variety of topics, and you must observe certain rules. Don't take chances!
- ☑ To provide better service, help customers, build loyalty, and prevent problems, you must monitor what people say about your brand or your products.
- ☑ Your ability to react and respond to a social media crisis before it gets out of control is critical.

The Future of Web Marketing

I never think of the future—it comes soon enough.

—Albert Einstein

People often ask me to predict the next big online thing. I try to stay connected to online journals, study blogs, and read technology magazines to get an assessment of where things might head online. If you make a habit of reading technology news sites like TechCrunch and Mashable, you'll be just about as educated as the so-called social media experts.

Most advancement online is predictable if you become deeply involved in getting to know this space. For example, you can probably predict several features of the next iPhone if you currently own one. However, every once in a while a social network or technology will come out of nowhere and explode on the scene. Such was the case with Pinterest, which is a visual social bookmarking site that encourages users to collect and share images and videos online.

It's a simple network, but it caught on quickly, and now is taking off faster than many of the famous social networks. In fact, Pinterest is now the number three most-popular social network in the United States, behind Facebook and Twitter, according to Experian Hitwise, a company that delivers the largest selection of daily insights on online consumer behaviors.

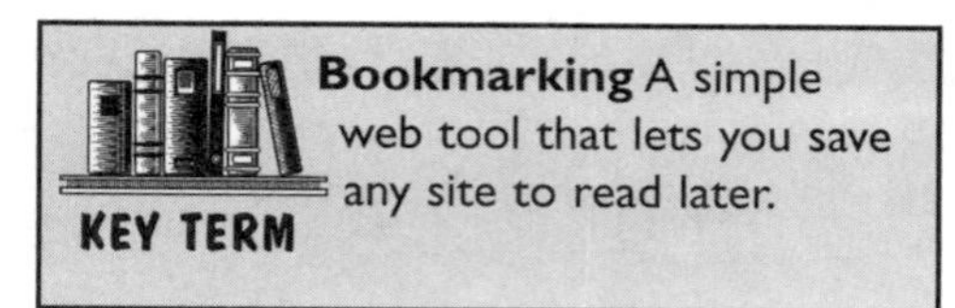

KEY TERM

Bookmarking A simple web tool that lets you save any site to read later.

THINK BEFORE YOU JUMP

The key to understanding a new network is, first, don't panic! For every new network that launches, several others fail. Make sure you gauge what your audience thinks of these new social networks before you invest time and money into marketing on them.

KEY TERM

Gamification The art of creating interactions through online or mobile applications that reward end users for their continuous involvement.

Gamification

Marketing professionals are always looking for low-cost ways to increase interaction with their target audience. This is why gamification has recently become so popular.

Gamification-based platforms tend to focus on rewarding users with nontangible items such as virtual badges, levels, mayorships, premium statuses, etc. These rewards are generally disseminated incrementally as a user interacts with the online platform—thereby encouraging ongoing use.

Gamification is impacting the ways businesses interact with customers, and even it's inspiring employees. By applying the same principles that motivate people to play games—achievement, status, rewards—businesses can increase audience size, drive engagement, increase revenues, and improve company morale.

At our company, Shoutlet, we reward innovation with mission badges—rewards given to employees for successfully completing specific assignments. The development team at Shoutlet is a group of top-notch coders, designers, and project managers. They work incredibly hard. For every new feature they create, there are a dozen being developed behind the scenes.

To recognize crew members who work on each in-depth project, the development team created badges. "We work so fast that it's a great way to recognize achievement in a way that's visible," said Jason Konen, director of development.

> **Game mechanics** Rules and feedback loops (continuous new information from users) intended to generate enjoyable gameplay. The mechanics consist of building blocks that can be applied and combined to gamify any nongame context.
>
> KEY TERM

More than 15 badges have been awarded over the past year. The badge stickers are highly coveted, both among the developers and the entire crew. On rare occasions, employees from other departments play a big enough role in the creation of a new feature that they receive a sticker, too.

What started as a fun way to acknowledge accomplishments has grown into a way to gamify the development process. Developers often say, "Put me on projects so I can earn a badge."

Gamification Examples

A popular example of gamification is Nike+. Nike successfully "gamified" exercise for everyone. When health becomes a competition, it seems a lot less like a doctor's order. Nike customers place a pedometer on a Nike sneaker and it monitors distance, pace, and calories burned, transmitting that data to the user's iPod. The Nike software loaded on the iPod rewards users when they reach a milestone. NikeFuel counts all the activities of the user's athletic life ranging from walking to basketball. Nike+ devices measure the user's moves, and he or she can compare and compete with anyone in the Nike+ community. The more the user moves, the more NikeFuel that user earns. When users do more exercise, they unlock virtual awards, trophies, and surprises. The whole idea kind of makes you want to start moving, doesn't it?

A couple of other timely examples include:

- Unlocking badges in Foursquare for visiting new or unique places.
- CrowdTap allows users to level up (advance to a new stage of the program) and earn money for doing surveys and other activities.

FarmVille is a Facebook social utility that connects people with friends and others who virtually work, study, and live around them. Players are able to give other FarmVille players gifts such as livestock or a tree. These gifts are free to give, and the clever part is that they invite reciprocity from the receiver. This encourages users to invite as many people as possible to join the game so they can all start exchanging gifts and kitting out their farms with more desirable objects. This viral element helps spread the use of FarmVille dramatically as people are actively encouraged to invite friends and provide gifts. Other than through this sharing, items in the game can be purchased with virtual cash, which players buy with real money. The most desirable items are usually affordable only with real money—a phenomenon that encourages players to spend on FarmVille.

The other key element to the gamification of FarmVille is the way it coaxes players. Meta games need to provide a reason for players to come back in order to promote long-term business. FarmVille does this by ensuring that if players do not actively return to their virtual farms, their crops will begin to die and their farm will fall apart—thereby depleting money, points, and status.

FOR EXAMPLE

EMPLOYEE RECOGNITION

Globoforce is a company that helps organizations build an extensive online reward system into their overall employee performance programs. Users of the Globoforce platform assume the position that recognition is strategic to a brand and the achievement of a company's goals. Globoforce's website (Globoforce.com) states, "Done right, recognition engages all employees and encourages them to recognize and appreciate coworkers every day." Their unique Strategic Recognition online software platform provides tools to identify key talent through online recognition rewards and track who is being recognized as well as who is giving recognition. Those online rewards can be cashed in for real incentives. The goal is to transform the fundamental nature of company culture. In effect, the program uses internal online marketing to engage a workforce.

Gamification is now recognized as one of the most effective methods of marketing today. Rarely have products or brands been able to exercise such control over consumer behavior, and this is why gamification and the use of meta games are employed across the Internet. Gamification is set to continue as an effective strategy to garner long-term consumer business and interest.

It's important to realize that gamification is expanding beyond media, restaurants, and fitness. The next predicted targets are e-commerce, education, local retail, and financial services. As I mentioned earlier, gamification

> **GAMIFICATION IN RESTAURANTS AND MEDIA**
>
> FOR EXAMPLE
>
> Restaurants take advantage of third-party systems like Foursquare to create specials for their restaurant, share deals with customers, etc. This is a form of gamification in that it provides rewards to the customer for being in a certain locale.
>
> Media uses gamification differently. For example, Pandora permits users to give a thumbs up or thumbs down rating to music.

is not only for consumers and end users, but also corporate employees. Corporations can gamify their products and services for consumers and end users, and they can also leverage game mechanics to make work more fun, measurable, productive, and rewarding for employees. Gamification can be oriented toward solo or social play, meeting a varying range of company needs. This might be something to add to your intranet to encourage employees to achieve objectives.

> **EMPLOYEE INCENTIVES**
>
> TOOLS
>
> One of Bunchball's fastest-growing products, called Nitro, allows companies such as SalesForce.com to incentivize employees to complete in an assortment of tasks. Nitro is a software platform that lets employers offer points to employees that are redeemable for such rewards as a dinner with the CEO or a new set of golf clubs.

Badges

Achievement awards have been around forever. Like the Boy Scouts and Girl Scouts, who earn badges for successful completion of an accomplishment or action. In today's environment of social media, badges are virtual, meaning you receive a digital image, e-mail, or text message once you have achieved a certain level or task on a social media site. Video gamers have years of exposure to these types of reward systems.

> **ENGAGING INTERNAL CUSTOMERS**
>
> SMART MANAGING
>
> You may wonder why I'd bother mentioning ways to engage employees in a book about online marketing. The reason is simple: When employees are engaged, they treat your customers better. Several studies point to the fact that employees are more productive when the culture is one of having fun and being rewarded. Your employees are your "internal customers." Engaging them helps them engage your customers.

Today, marketers are integrating badges into loyalty programs, contests, and everyday shopping experiences. There is a certain level of accomplishment a person feels when earning another badge. Marketers play on this psychological phenomenon by leveraging achievement with engagement.

FUNCTIONS FOR BADGES

Goal setting Badges challenge participants or employees to reach a goal or accomplish a task that is set for them. Goal setting is known to be an effective motivator.

Instruction Badges provide instruction about what types of activity are possible or permissable within a given system. Badges can be used as a game mechanic to encourage participants to take a specific action (like visit 10 Mexican restaurants or check in at a certain location, etc.).

Reputation An identifying badge by which users get feedback on their actions; it can provide information to make reputation assessments. These badges encapsulate a user's interests, expertise, and past interactions. To encourage this sort of constant interaction, the start-up CrowdTwist has built a software platform that allows businesses to offer its users points for a variety of tasks, from "liking" the company on Facebook to reading the company's blog. The points have real-life rewards. In one example, CrowdTwist's software was used by a music festival that let high scorers win prizes like dinner with their favorite band or being serenaded on stage. For leaving positive reviews, etc., brands can reward their customers.

Status/affirmation Badges are motivating as status symbols. They advertise one's achievements and communicate one's past accomplishments without explicit bragging.

Group identification Badges communicate a set of shared activities that bind a group of participants together around shared experience. Achieving badges provides a sense of solidarity and increases positive group identification.

Source: Antin, J.; Churchill, E. F., "Badges in Social Media: A Social Psychological Perspective," research.yahoo.com/node/3469.

Business Value of Gamification

It's easy to focus on how engaging a game's features and functions are, and clearly it's important to keep users engaged and coming back for more. Initially, it is common for organizations to focus on the gaming mechanics of their site and how to make the site more fun and engaging for users.

The business value to the company implementing gamification is in understanding the behavioral science behind the experience. The value is to study and understand the customers' actions—their knowledge, interests, likes, and dislikes. Organizations employ that information to better profile users and understand how gamification impacts use of their products/services and, more important, what users are interested in. Gamification applications allow those companies that use them to observe customer patterns, which translate into valuable measurement tools.

Some organizations think of gamification as simply adding a few badges to one area of a website with no social context. Or they use the wrong game mechanics for their particular user experience and demographic—such as one that wouldn't likely engage the target audience because it appeals to a different age or interest group.

Gamification will undoubtedly become one of the next big trends. While adding a few badges to a site to reward a handful of behaviors may motivate limited behavior immediately, it likely will not have any sustainable long-term impact on your business objectives. Status and virtual rewards are only as valuable as the community in which they are awarded and displayed. Smart gamification requires a deep integration of a rewards program across a brand's entire user experience. It is all about sustainable business results, using techniques to influence customer and employee behavior. We will see companies expect gamification's usefulness to be proven by real results and ROI.

The Future of Gaming

In the future, enterprises will take greater advantage of sophisticated gamification techniques to monitor and reward employees who go through corporate training programs and update their certifications. In addition to training compliance, enterprises will likely increase their focus on rewarding employees for a variety of desirable behaviors, including helping achieve sales, product development, and other relevant goals.

Virtual Worlds and Social Game Advertising

An unexplored digital terrain for advertisers includes the innovative virtual worlds.

Second Life is a 3-D virtual world where users can socialize, connect, and create using free voice and text chat. Entropia Universe is an advanced 3-D online virtual environment with a developed planetary system and one universal Real Cash Economy system. Each planet offers a wide variety of exciting entertainment. A user can travel among the planets and socialize with people from all over the world.

Second Life and Entropia Universe give users an opportunity to communicate and engage in ways unattainable through other media. In these platforms, users create 3-D *avatars* (human or fantasy characters) that can walk, fly, or teleport to navigate virtual new worlds. Real money is used in these virtual landscapes, and the border between what is real versus imagined is fuzzy. Users may bond and create groups based on shared interests. Companies may create virtual worlds or platforms that attract specific users and integrate their brands into the landscape.

This makes me pause and wonder, could virtual worlds be the next big medium for advertising? When consumers are online, studies show that the average American spends more time on Facebook than on Google, Yahoo, YouTube, Microsoft, Wikipedia, and Amazon combined. A significant part of that interaction includes social games, making them an ideal alternative to display ads for advertisers who want to reach Face-

FOR EXAMPLE

FARMVILLE MEETS MARKETING

According to Mashable—a popular site that follows social media news, tools, and trends—the most popular Facebook social game, FarmVille, had for the first time an option to plant a specific branded crop on their virtual farms. In more than 500 million cases, players chose to buy and plant the branded blueberries instead of something else. According to Zynga, unaided brand awareness increased 550 percent as a result of this user interaction.

(Zynga is a provider of social game services. The company develops games that work both stand-alone on mobile phone platforms such as Apple iOS and Android and as application widgets on its website, Zynga.com, and social networking websites such as Facebook, Google+, and Tencent. Zynga mission is "Connecting the world through games.")

book's giant, 1 billion-person user base (mashable.com/2010/12/05/social-games-advertising).

Volvo, H&M, and MTV Networks have experimented with branded virtual goods that users can choose to purchase or acquire through interaction with the brand. Another common strategy for brands in social games is an *offer wall* inside many games. Brands can exchange virtual rewards for engagement, like taking a survey or watching a video about a new product.

The majority of social games are free to play and fairly easy to learn. In virtual world games, brands can do more than be displayed on billboards (though that is an option, too). The brands can also become part of the game and the overall experience.

One way brands have successfully become a part of the game is by adding a game element. For example, in 2010 Farmers Insurance paid to brand a blimp in the FarmVille game, and players who chose to put it on their farms had their crops protected during the 10 days of the promotion. The branded blimp continued to float over their farms even after the promotion ended. Marc Zeitlin, vice president of e-business for Farmers Insurance, said, "Millions of Farmers Airships were placed on FarmVille farms. FarmVille players were exposed to the Farmers brand billions of times, raising our Facebook fan base by more than 100,000 in the first week of the promotion. It was one of the most successful things we've done from a branding perspective" (bizjournals.com/seattle/blog/techflash/2011/06/farmers-insurance-returns-to-farmville.html).

VIRTUAL WORLDS

TOOLS

The following sites offer virtual worlds for users:

- Second Life (secondlife.com)
- Active Worlds (activeworlds.com)
- Blue Mars (bluemars.com)
- Cloud Party (cloudpartytime.com)
- Club Cooee (clubcooee.com)
- Football Superstars (footballsuperstars.com)
- Free Realms (freerealms.com)
- Frenzoo (frenzoo.com)
- Friends Hangout (friendshangout.com)

Dynamic Content Generation and Targeting

Marketers are not only becoming more involved in the content creation process, they have also realized that repurposing content created for a specific demographic or channel is unsustainable long-term.

As customer expectations grow, relevant content that is personalized in real time—meaning it is relevant to the current moment—gradually becomes the norm for forward-thinking brands. As mobile usage grows, companies have adapted content to a wide range of devices. The rise of smartphones and smart devices like tablets are changing how consumers interact with organizations, while also raising customers' expectations for accessing an organization's services anywhere and any time.

Despite the growing popularity of mobile devices, organizations have been slow to react. According to recent Econsultany research, mobile is low on organizations' priority list, with only 29 percent of client-side respondents reporting this to be a top 2012 priority.

So, what is the future of web marketing? Judging from various studies, if you haven't started thinking about how your site looks on a smartphone or an iPad, then you are already behind the curve.

TOOLS

Passbook

Passbook keeps things like airline boarding passes, movie tickets, and gift cards all in one place. Everything's there—ready for scanning—right from your iPhone. You'll find Passbook-enabled apps on the App Store.

Passbook is time and location based, so your passes and tickets automatically appear when and where you need them. Arrive at the airport and your boarding pass pops up. If you're waiting to board the flight and your gate changes, Passbook tells you. And if you decide to grab a coffee on the way to your new gate, your gift card appears when you walk into the cafe.

Starbucks recently updated its iPhone app with iOS 6 compatibility, and it includes Passbook integration. With this integration, users receive a Passbook alert when their balance updates, and any changes made to locations or card information is synced automatically to Passbook. There's a right way to integrate an app or service with Passbook, and it's clear Starbucks is doing it the right way.

Location-Based Marketing

Location-based apps—those that react to a user's specific location and provide customized information—offer benefits such as navigation, location-based discounts, connecting with others by proximity (who is near the user at a given time), and social information-sharing through features like check-ins. Imagine you are at your fitness club and you "check in" via a smartphone. You can see which friends are at the club now, and perhaps the more you visit the club, the bigger discount you will get on next year's membership. The potential for leveraging location data is truly limitless. That same gym check-in could also show you the history of your club usage, plan your workout programs, track your diet, and link up with heart-rate monitors and wearable sensors to communicate wirelessly with treadmills and other equipment.

ScreenScape, a provider of location-based media, has been providing digital signage solutions (digital advertising combined with dynamic content based on a user's location) for many venues including fitness clubs. Mark Hemphill, founder and COO of ScreenScape, says that "place-based media is a natural fit for fitness clubs. There are tons of applications ranging from fitness videos to membership drives and loyalty programs that make it a natural application for both venue enhancement and member engagement."

In a recent article, *AdWeek* claimed that we'll be seeing more of this type of geotargeting technology taken to a whole new level. *AdWeek* mentioned bus shelter posters that change instantly to offer you a free coffee as you walk by or cereal coupons that pop up when you hit the cereal aisle at the store. It's not only about location; it's also about timing. Location and timing combined clearly create a powerful advertising jackpot. This concept is referred to as *geofencing* (see adweek.com/news/technology/where-are-you-going-where-have-you-been-138178).

Check-in services—meaning those in which a user "checks in" virtually to a specific geographic location, typically via a mobile device—are the most common use of location-based advertising, and require an initial app download and continual updates. Geofencing reaches out to the consumer who doesn't have to do anything but click on the opportunity presented on the screen. The geofencing technology could potentially scan your smartphone as you stroll by the ad (see adweek.com/news/technology/where-are-you-going-where-have-you-been-138178 for more).

When you're marketing your restaurant, for example, you want to identify hungry people near your location in Chicago. That targeting narrows the reach of your campaign. The upside? When you target by location, you're not paying for people on the north side to see an ad for a restaurant on the south side.

Location-Based Interactions

TOOLS

Location-based interactions know and keep track of user preferences when users interact with a brand. Note these key points about location-based interactions:

- Location-based interactions are examples of personalized, premise-based marketing.
- Belly App is an example of location-based marketing (see Bellycard .com).
- Interactions go beyond Foursquare; they can remember your preferences and give you points that meet your needs. For example, Belly Apps or the Bare Minerals Fab Friend card give you a gift based on your makeup preferences (bareescentuals.com/on/demandware.store /Sites-BareEscentuals-Site/default/FABMarketing-Start)

TRICKS OF THE TRADE

Adapting to Changes in Privacy

Not surprisingly, consumers' biggest worry is privacy. As much as we like the convenience of having targeted coupons and ads, we don't like the idea of being tracked and followed. As we move forward with technology, it's likely that location tracking will be as common as a listed phone number. Our notions of privacy are evolving and changing. And oddly, the majority of users are okay with that.

Aaron Strout, coauthor of *Location-Based Marketing for Dummies* with Mike Schneider, said that,

> B2B and B2C, media, supply chain management, etc., can all benefit from reaching their key stakeholders at the right place and the right time. With that said, they agree that location-based marketing is obviously low hanging fruit for retailers and small businesses that own their physical locations. In particular, those that have high foot

traffic can benefit the most through deals, recognition programs, experiential opportunities and other elements that build loyalty.

Strout and Schneider say that the "must-haves" of any good location-based marketing program are to:

1. Set goals
2. Have a compelling offer
3. Operationalize

At the end of the day, smart marketers win. The rate of change in location-based marketing presents both opportunities and challenges for brands, and knowing the popular trends in location-based marketing is key to ensuring that today's decisions turn into tomorrow's successes for your company.

Manager's Checklist for Chapter 11

☑ Gamification is a great way to motivate people to become and stay engaged and create interactions that don't require payments.

☑ Use badges for employee goal setting and rewards for accomplishments achieved internally—improving your employee engagement, which translates to building greater customer loyalty.

☑ Dynamic content helps create unique user interactions in a way that is nondisruptive to the user experience.

☑ Companies can now reach out to audiences on a local level. Localization is an increasingly powerful tactic as social networks strengthen their technology.

☑ Location-based marketing uses technologies like Foursquare to create in-person or "on location" interactions.

Staying Ahead of the Curve

You can observe a lot just by watching.

—Yogi Berra, former baseball player and manager

Many clients I work with seem amazed by how much knowledge I have about online marketing and social media. My employees and friends even believe I have some sort of crystal ball that helps me predict online trends. The truth is that I like to read. I'm passionate about the industry I work in, so my thirst for information is never ending.

Maneuverability: Don't Build on Rented Land

Remember Friendster? How about MySpace? Now that Facebook controls about 80 percent of the World Wide Web, we have quickly forgotten about the social networks that came before it.

Friendster, launched in 2002, was one of the first social networking sites to attain more than 1 million members. Friendster allowed people to create personal pages and connect to others in a LinkedIn fashion but without the business ties. Interestingly, in 2003, Friendster management received a $30 million buyout offer from Google, which they declined. But Friendster's computer systems couldn't keep up with the explosive growth (reportedly due to the complexity of the security model set up to control connections, privacy, and authenticity of users), so in 2004 MySpace

Change Direction or Perish

My good friend used to be a tank operator in the Swedish Army. He told me a story about his work and how important "maneuverability" is when you're in battle. "If you don't have a way to change direction quickly, you're dead," he said. It's like that in the digital world. The only constant is change, and to remain viable, you must be maneuverable.

swept up the market in a landslide (techcrunch.com/2010/2/04/social-networking-present).

MySpace was growing at the same time we all had cheap digital cameras, smartphones, and video cameras like the Flip that let us create videos. Unfortunately, MySpace couldn't handle or hold images or video successfully. Photobucket and ImageShack functioned well, and MySpace users put all their photos on Photobucket and their videos on YouTube, easily sharing them with their friends through the MySpace interface. Fox bought MySpace for $580 million and then did a deal with Google worth more than the purchase price to serve up ads. Google then acquired YouTube for $1.65 billion, and successfully transformed YouTube into one of the most valuable Internet properties. MySpace later bought Photobucket for $250 million plus a $50 million earn out. It did not have the same success as Google's acquisition and MySpace sold Photobucket two years later to a relatively unknown Seattle-based start-up called Ontela for a reported $60 million.

Then came Facebook. The social networking website was launched on February 4, 2004. It grew rapidly between 2004 and 2007 to 100 million users, which was actually fewer users than MySpace had at the time.

Facebook was everything that MySpace wasn't. It was exclusive for college students, visually pleasing, easy to use, ad-free, and users were verified. MySpace was middle-America, targeted for teenagers with a design that was frenzied, and on heavy on advertising. According to *The Wall Street Journal*'s October 4, 2012 article, "One Billion and Counting," Facebook had more than 1 billion active users, more than half of them using Facebook on a mobile device.

While Facebook was built on the idea that all our information should be kept private and shared only among friends, Twitter was designed to share information with anyone. Twitter was created in March 2006 and launched that July. The service rapidly gained worldwide popularity, with more than 500 million active users as of 2012, generating over 340 million tweets daily and performing more than 1.6 billion search queries per day (media bistro.com/alltwitter/500-million-registered-users_b18842). This was a revolutionary innovation in social thinking, and it was effective. Twitter connects people of all backgrounds and interests, allowing users to filter their news feed to include only people they find interesting. Twitter restricts each post to 140 characters, which encourages users to share links with other people—one of the unique features of Twitter (en.wiki pedia.org/wiki/Twitter).

It's clear that our perception of privacy is constantly evolving. If we could time travel back to our state of mind several years ago, I think many of us would be stunned by our social media behaviors now. As the digital era progresses, we'll continue to feel more comfortable and confident about sharing most aspects of our lives.

Cisco and Old Spice ROI

FOR EXAMPLE

Providing an alternative view of social media's ROI, a Cisco case study illustrates how social technologies saved them more than $100,000 during a product launch. Instead of their costly traditional product launch practice, which involved flying in high-profile execs and running expensive print ads, they used social media to run an entirely online campaign. They staged a pre-launch concert. This entire launch was less expensive (one-sixth of the cost) as well as more expansive in its reach than their traditional launches.

To fully understand the value of a social media campaign and its effect on ROI, review one of the most famous and successful social media campaigns: Old Spice. Through their campaign, which included sending personalized video messages to social media fans and celebrities, they gathered statistics on the response. The reach was clear, but what about sales?

> Since the original campaign launched with "Mustafa," sales increased by 27% year on year. But in the 3 months after the height of the campaign, sales were up by 55%, reaching 107% in the final month of the social media campaign. And of course, Old Spice is now the number 1 body wash brand for men. However you choose to look at the campaign, these figures stand up to show that a social media campaign, well executed, can drive significant ROI for your business" (thenextweb..com/socialmedia/2011/07/16/the-roi-of-social-media-10-case-studies).

To remain competitive in this digital era we live in, businesses must keep up with the times and the evolving space of online platforms. Your online presence and brand reputation are hugely important in the eyes of potential customers, competitors, and shareholders. Studies continue to prove how social media sites translate to profit. Creating social media sites for your business is no longer an option—it's a necessity.

Resources for Staying up to Speed

Social networking is increasingly mobile, and that adds a new perspective on how we leverage social media connections. The most obvious change is that now social networks are location focused. The highest-profile application in this space is Foursquare, which focuses on connecting people through proximity.

FOR EXAMPLE

GOING MOBILE

According to a report from Juniper Research, more than 1.3 billion users are expected to access social media from mobile devices by 2016. This is almost double the number of mobile social media users in 2011. The report found "the trend to integrate social, local, and mobile experiences is driving the geosocial phenomena. People want to find out not only what their friends are doing, but also their location and other available activities in the area."

FOR EXAMPLE

FACEBOOK USERS ON THE GO

Facebook "expects its next 1 billion users to come mainly from mobile devices, rather than desktop computers," according to a recent financialpost.com report by tech desk editor Matt Hartley in "Facebook's Looming Mobile Conundrum" (business.financialpost.com/2012/02/02/facebooks-looming-mobile-conundrum).

The mobile space is accessible to geosocial networks as most smartphones now include GPS features.

This also means digital content strategies for mobile social media will have to be reconstructed based on how content is used on these platforms.

What is interesting about the social media future is how it will transform our online behavior. Users are learning about, adapting to, and growing more aware of their surroundings. Photos and video are also playing more prominent roles in how we communicate and share information.

At present, Pinterest is particularly interesting because of what people "pin" and how they share and comment on pinned items on social media sites like Facebook. It's creating new reasons for interactions and creating new behaviors and mindsets. Pinterest is a great resource for businesses. In fact, the site is driving high levels of traffic to retailer websites, and early data indicate that the website is directly linked to sales. Clearly, there are beneficial effects of strong "pinfluence" (articles.latimes .com/2012/apr/12/business/la-fi-pinterest-20120413).

The greatest takeaway for companies is that we must all adapt to this new social and digital realm. Essentially, it's time to sink or swim. What are you waiting for? Don't be afraid to jump in the water and get your feet wet. You might even make a splash.

Online Marketing Resources

TOOLS

Here are some resources for staying ahead of the digital curve:

- HOW TO: Optimize marketing copy for mobile, mashable.com/2011/06/14/optimize-mobile-marketing/
- Social media marketing for dummies (cheat sheet), www.dummies.com/how-to/content/social-media-marketing-for-dummies-cheat-sheet.html
- Social media webinars, us.cision.com/events/webinars.asp
- Tech crunch, techcrunch.com

Source: techcrunch.com/2010/12/05/social-networking-future

Mobile Marketing Association

TRICKS OF THE TRADE

The Mobile Marketing Association is a valuable resource for brands.

> The Mobile Marketing Association (MMA) is the premier global non-profit trade association representing all players in the mobile marketing value chain. With more than 700 member companies, the MMA is an action-oriented organization with global focus, regional actions and local relevance. The MMA's primary focus is to establish mobile as an indispensable part of the marketing mix. MMA members include agencies, advertisers, hand held device manufacturers, carriers and operators, retailers, software providers and service providers, as well as any company focused on the potential of marketing via mobile devices (mmaglobal.com).

Manager's Checklist for Chapter 12

- ☑ The only constant in the digital world is change.
- ☑ Our notions of privacy are in flux.
- ☑ Social networking is becoming mobile, increasing the ways we use the platforms.
- ☑ Online behavior is evolving. Photos and videos now play a role in how we communicate and share information.

Index

About the Author

Jason Weaver is founder and CEO of Shoutlet, a leading social media marketing platform used by global brands, small businesses, and marketing agencies to build, engage, and measure their social media communication. Jason is considered an authority in social media with more than 15 years experience as an entrepreneur, executive, and innovator. In 2002, years before the launch of Facebook and Twitter, he discovered the power of working collaboratively through social networks to help execute engagement-marketing campaigns within online communities. As a social media thought leader, Jason has provided strategic expertise to companies including Disney, eBay, and SC Johnson on their social media strategies. He is a much sought after author and speaker for organizations such as the American Marketing Association, Public Relations Society of America, and American Advertising Federation. To learn more, visit shoutlet.com.